GU00865050

Ten Minutes To Curtain!
BY
TRISHA SUGAREK

A COLLECTION OF SHORT PLAYS FOR
THE YOUNG ACTOR

Made in the U.S.A.
All rights reserved.
ISBN 978-1449904272

NOTICE

Copyright PAu2-931-334. Trisha Sugarek, 2011. This book is offered for sale at the price quoted only with the understanding that, if any additional copies of the whole or any part are necessary for its production, such additional copies will be purchased. The attention of all purchasers is directed to the following: this work is fully protected under the copyright laws of the United States of America, the British Commonwealth, including Canada, and all other countries of the Copyright Union. Violations of the Copyright Law are punishable by fine or imprisonment, or both. Single copies of plays are sold for reading purposes only. The copying or duplicating of a play, or any part of the play, by hand or by any other process, is an infringement of the copyright. Such infringement will be vigorously prosecuted.

These plays may not be produced by amateurs or professionals for public or private performance without first submitting application for performing rights. Royalties are due on all performances whether for charity or gain, or whether admission is charged or not since performance of this play without the payment of the royalty fee renders anybody participating liable to severe penalties imposed by the law, anybody acting in this play should be certain, before doing so, that the royalty fee has been paid. Professional rights, reading rights, radio broadcasting, television and all mechanical rights, etc., are strictly reserved. **Application for performing rights should be made directly to the playwright, Trisha Sugarek, at www.writeratplay.com.** No one shall commit or authorize any act or omission by which the copyright of, or the right to copyright, this play may be impaired. No one shall make any changes in these plays for the purpose of production. Publication of these plays does not imply availability for performance. Both amateurs and professionals considering a production of one or more are strongly advised in their interest to apply to Trisha Sugarek for written permission before starting rehearsals, advertising, or booking a theatre.

Whenever the plays are produced, the author's name must be carried in all publicity, advertising, posters, and programs. Also, the following notice must appear on all printed programs, 'Produced by special arrangement with the Playwright, Trisha Sugarek.'

Also by
TRISHA SUGAREK

<u>ShortN'Small * Series (short plays/small casts)</u>

Toe Tag #47
The Ash Can
The Waltz
The Bullies
Curiosity Killed the Cat
A Hint of Magnolia
Love Never Leaves Bruises
Great Expectations
The Perfume Bottle
Straight Edged Secret
Orange Socks
You're Not the Boss of Me!
The 'D' Word
Mean Girls
Training the Troops
Daughterland
The Bard of the Yukon
You're Fat, You're Ugly and You Dress Weird
Cyber-Hate
Forever Yours
The Last Text
TradeLies.com
If We Break Up, I'll Die!
Mr. Churchill's Cat
A Dime Bag of Weed
The Art of Murder
The Run-Away
The Wedding Crasher
Trans-G Kid
Trans-G Parents

CONTENTS

The Bullies

Cast of Characters

Aamir........A teen born in the USA, his family is from India.
In his first year of high school, he is on the varsity debate team and a
state champion in Chess.

Taggart "Tag"….A junior in high school, a football star, and a bully.

Steve……One of Tag's friends and followers.

Jimmy… Another friend of Tag's, a football linebacker. He reluctantly follows the gang but his
instincts tell him that bullying is not right.

Voice Off. (Dr. Chandak)…Aamir's father is a physicist and came to the US before Aamir was
born. He has a very slight accent in his speech patterns.

Scene One

At Rise: Friday afternoon after school. A table, a chair and a computer.

*(**AAMIR** sits in front of a computer screen working on homework. A bell sounds that   a message is coming in. **AAMIR** clicks on the window.)*

AAMIR. *(reads aloud)* 'We know you're a terrorist so go back to where you come from.   We don't want your filth in our town.' *(Shocked he closes the message with a click.)* Wow! That was bizarre-o! Wonder where that came from.

*(Another ding. **AAMIR** stares at the computer screen. **HE** doesn't open the email.)*

*(Across the stage, three boys are grouped around a computer. **TAGGERT** is at the keyboard. **STEVE** and **JIMMY** are laughing..)*

STEVE.   Write another one, Tag.
TAG. *(laughing)* The little faggot opened that one. Here's a new one.

*(Typing, **TAG** reads what he's written out loud to **HIS** friends.)*

TAG. We don't want you Muslim slant-eyes in our country. Go home! If you don't, you'll be sorry. *(Clicks send.)*

*(**STEVE** and **TAG** laugh uproariously. **JIMMY** laughs half-heartedly.)*

JIMMY. Hey, guys! This is boring. Let's go throw a football around.
TAG. Are you nuts? This is the best fun I've had all week. *(laughs)* It is our duty, as US citizens to root out evil wherever we find it! *(begins to type again)* Let's see how he likes this one. *(reading aloud)* You better not be in school on Monday. We'll be waiting for you. We got a little surprise for you that you won't like.
STEVE. Oh yeah, that'll scare the crap outta the little four-eyes.

*(**AAMIR** opens the two new emails. **HE** reads them to **HIMSELF**. **HE** makes a disgusted noise and closes the window.)*

AAMIR. *(muttering)* What a bunch of sicko's.   You'd think that they would have better things to do.

VOICE Off. (Dr. Chandak) Aamir, come on, we will be late for your chess competition. Traffic will be bad. Hurry, now.

AAMIR. Coming, Dad.

(AAMIR exits.)

Scene Two

At Rise: Sunday afternoon.

*(**AAMIR** sits at the table, text books around **HIS** computer. An alert sound that there is a new email.)*

AAMIR.*(sighing)* What now?

*(**HE** clicks on the window. **HE** reads the message and then begins typing furiously.)*

AAMIR. Who are you?

*(Across the stage **TAG** sits at **HIS** computer and types back, reading aloud as **HE** types.)*

TAG. Your worst nightmare. Ready for school tomorrow, douche-bag?

*(Across the stage, **AAMIR** reads the message and begins to type. **THEY** read aloud.)*

AAMIR. *(typing)* Who are you!?
TAG. *(typing)* You'll find out if you've got the cachones to come to school tomorrow.
AAMIR. *(typing)* I'm not afraid of you. You're a coward, you know that? Hiding behind a computer.
TAG. *(typing)* We'll see who's the coward when you go running away screaming like a little girl. See ya tomorrow, slant-eyes.

*(Simultaneously, both **BOYS** close down **THEIR** computers.)*

VOICE Off. (Dr. Chandak) Aamir! Come down now, dinner is prepared.
AAMIR. *(Rises and crosses to the door.)* I'm not hungry, Dad. I'll eat later.
VOICE Off. (Dr. Chandak) You will come now, son. Your mother worked ever so hard to prepare a family feast. You will not disappoint her.
AAMIR. (s*ighing*) Be right down, Dad.

Scene Three

At Rise: The next day at school.

(AAMIR is walking to HIS next class. TAG, STEVE and JIMMY are walking toward AAMIR. As the BOYS pass each other, TAG bumps into AAMIR hard.)

AAMIR. *(polite)* Oh, sorry. Guess I wasn't watching where I was going.

(AAMIR tries to walk on. The three other BOYS surround HIM.)

TAG. You talkin' to me, sand-nigger?

(STEVE giggles nervously at the 'n' word and JIMMY gasps at how far TAG is taking this.)

TAG. *(shoving Aamir again)* Answer me, boy!
AAMIR. You're him….the one that's been sending me emails.
TAG. *(laughing, he turns to his buddies)* The guy's a genius, figured it out all by himself that it was us.

(Not to be left out, STEVE punches AAMIR on the arm.)

STEVE A real genius. Pretty smart for a black boy.
AAMIR. I am not African-American, I am Indian.

(TAG begins to hoot and holler and starts what HE believes to be a Native-American dance. STEVE follows HIS lead. JIMMY stands off to the side watching. AAMIR starts to walk off.)

TAG. Hey! Where ya goin'? Did I say you could leave?

(TAG blocks AAMIR's path.)

AAMIR. I will be late for class.
TAG. Oh, boo-hoo, he's going to be late for class.
JIMMY. So are we, Tag. We can't be late again or we'll be benched Friday night.
TAG. *(whirling on his friend)* Did I ask you for your opinion?
JIMMY. No.

STEVE. But, he's right, Tag. Coach warned us.

TAG. Yeah, like Coach is gonna bench *me*, the starting quarterback? Riiiight!

*(**TAG** turns to **AAMIR** and punch-shoves **HIM** in the chest. **AAMIR**'s books go flying. The **BOYS** laugh.)*

TAG. Ya got off easy this time, 'Genius'. Scamper off to class like a good little gook.

*(The three **BULLIES** saunter off, laughing. **AAMIR** picks **HIS** books off the ground and walks away in the opposite direction.)*

Later that day **AAMIR** sits at his computer. **HIS** cell phone rings.

AAMIR. Hello? Oh, Hi, Derek. What're you doing? No I haven't been on FaceBook for a couple of days, why? *(Beat.)* Really? About me? Hold on. *(clicks and types as HE talks)* ... I'm bringing it up now. Whose wall?.....OK.

*(**AAMIR** reads aloud while his friend waits on the phone.)*

AAMIR. 'A terrorist just waiting to strike'? 'A secret Muslim cell right here in our midst'? *(listens to his friend)*... No, of course it's not true. Gosh, Derek, you've known me since fourth grade. Besides, I'm not even Saudi Arabian or Afganistanian, I'm Indian.....I'm not even Muslim. *(listening)*...I don't know what I'm going to do. Probably just ignore it......Yeah, catch ya later, bye.

*(**AAMIR** sits, staring at **HIS** computer screen.)*

Scene Four

At Rise: Later that week, at the end of the school day.

(AAMIR is walking to the room where his chess club meets. HE is carrying the box that holds his chess pieces. TAG, STEVE and   JIMMY are waiting around a corner. As AAMIR walks by THEY jump out and surround AAMIR. TAG knocks the box out of AAMIR's hands and scoops it up.)

AAMIR. *(grabbing for the box)* Hey! That's mine. Give it back.
TAG. Not anymore it ain't.
STEVE. Yeah, it's ours now.

(TAG opens the box, all the time avoiding AAMIR's attempts to get it back. TAG pulls out a very beautiful,wood carved chess piece.)

AAMIR. Don't touch those.
STEVE. Who's gonna stop us?\
TAG. Hey, guys, look at the little statue. What does the Bible say about graven images? You worship graven images back in the jungles where you come from, four-eyes?
AAMIR. Those are chess pieces, Taggart. *Not* graven images. Now give them back!
TAG. Why should I?
STEVE. Yeah, why should he?
JIMMY. Come on, Tag, give 'em back. We're gonna be late for practice.
TAG. Shut up, Jimmy. *(To Aamir.)* So what's the deal? Is this where you hide the explosives? Let's crack one open and see.
STEVE. Yeah.
AAMIR. NO! My father gave me that chess set.

(It is AAMIR's prize possession. AAMIR makes a grab for the box and inadvertently strikes TAG in the chest. EVERYONE is absolutely still for a beat. TAG tosses the box to STEVE and rushes AAMIR.)

TAG. Did you just hit me, ya little faggot?

(TAG begins to strike AAMIR in the face and body. AAMIR tries to cover HIS face and falls to the ground and curls up. As TAG hits AAMIR.)

TAG. Huh? You want to fight me?? You got it, ya little douche-bag! *(punch)* Gook! *(punch)* Slant-eyes! *(punch)* You don't belong here. America is for Americans!

(TAG doesn't appear to be able to stop hitting. JIMMY pulls HIM off of AAMIR.)

JIMMY. Tag! That's enough. Cut it out! We're gonna get into trouble. Come on, stop!

(JIMMY pulls TAG away. AAMIR stays on the ground. TAG straightens HIS clothes and swaggers over to STEVE. HE takes the box from STEVE and throws it down on top of AAMIR. Chess pieces scatter everywhere.)

TAG. Come on, guys, let's get outta here. I gotta wash my hands after touching this faggot.

(TAG and STEVE saunter off, laughing together as THEY exit. JIMMY has stayed behind. Slowly, JIMMY begins to pick up the chess pieces and puts them   back into the box. AAMIR sits up and when HE sees that only JIMMY remains, HE stands. JIMMY hands   the box to AMMIR.)

JIMMY. Here, I'm not sure I found them all.

(AAMIR checks the pieces in the box.)

AAMIR. There's two missing.

(The BOYS look around and each find one of the missing pieces. JIMMY hands the piece he found to AAMIR.)

AAMIR. Thanks.
JIMMY. Welcome. *(Beat)* Your cheek is bleeding.

(AAMIR takes out a white handkerchief and wipes HIS face.)

Does it hurt?
AAMIR. Not too much. But my ribs hurt like the devil.

(JIMMY laughs nervously. And after a moment, AAMIR joins in.)

AAMIR. *(holding his side)* Oww! Laughing hurts.
JIMMY. Look. I'm sorry, okay? This got way out of hand.
AAMIR. Yeah.
JIMMY. We were just horsing around on the computer, teasing guys, not just you. Then, well, Tag….I don't know….he kinda got all focused on you for some reason. *(beat)* I'm sorry you got beat up. I had no idea it was going to go this far.
AAMIR. I'm not a terrorist.
JIMMY. I know. Tag just made that up.
AAMIR. Why me? Abdallah and Nadim both go to our school and they're from Saudi.
JIMMY. Yeah, except they're…

AAMIR. Football players.

JIMMY. And bigger than Tag. I don't think he would mess with *them*. *(Beat)* Are you going to report this to the office?

AAMIR. And be a snitch besides being a terrorist?

> *(**THEY** both laugh.)*

I don't think so. I'm so clumsy, I keep running into locker doors.

JIMMY. I just want you to know that I was pretty uncomfortable with some of the names Tag called you. That's not what I think at all.

AAMIR. Yeah, I know. Where'd he learn all that hate?

JIMMY. His Dad, I think. The first time his Dad saw Abdallah and Nadim at practice he went ballistic. He threatened to pull Tag off the football team. He fought in Desert Storm, whatever that is. He called them a lot of the names Tag called you. It was crazy, man.

> *(Beat. Looks at **HIS** watch.)*

Jeesch, look at the time, I'm am so late. Coach is gonna kill me!

AAMIR. Yeah, me too. I didn't mean…not the coach….the chess club, I mean. They are so punctual.

> *(**THEY** laugh again and **JIMMY** puts his hand out to shake.*
>
> ***AAMIR** looks at it and then shakes **JIMMY**'s hand. **THEY** grin at each other over the hand shake.)*

JIMMY. No hard feelings?

AAMIR. Nah. See ya around.

JIMMY. Yeah, see ya.

> *(**THEY** walk off in separate directions.)*

Scene Five

At Rise: A few weeks later. A room at school.

(JIMMY is working on some poster board at a table as AAMIR enters. Walking up HE looks over JIMMY's shoulder.)

AAMIR Wow! Look at that!
JIMMY. What do you think?
AAMIR. Do your jock friends know that you're such a good artist?
JIMMY. Gosh, no. Do you think I want to get beat up?

(As THEY laugh together, JIMMY holds up the poster. It is an almost completed poster that reads: `'STUDENTS AGAINST VIOLENCE! Stop the Bullying NOW!')`

AAMIR. I just talked to two more kids that want to join our anti-violence program.
JIMMY. How many does that make now?
AAMIR. Sixty-four at last count. And Principal Anderson is going to let us speak at the next student assembly.
JIMMY. I'll leave the speaking to you.
AAMIR. And I'll leave the drawing to you.
JIMMY. Deal. (la*ughing*) You can't draw a straight line.
AAMIR. It sure didn't hurt our cause when Tiffany joined. She's only about the most popular girl in the entire school district. Who would have thought that she was bullied in grade school?
JIMMY. Go figure. She's so smart and pretty. What kind'a creep would bully her? *(beat)* Did you hear? Tag asked Tiffany to the prom and she turned him down. Told him she didn't date bullies.
AAMIR. No joke? What did Tag do?
JIMMY. He just puffed up and told her he'd only asked her on a dare. Tiff laughed in his face.
AAMIR. *(pumps his fist in the air)* Go! Tiffany!
JIMMY. I heard it from Tiff's best friend, Jill who was there. She's in my chem class. *(beat)* Are Tag and Steve leaving you alone, Aamir?
AAMIR. Oh yeah. *(laughing)* I guess my black eye and scabby face scared them off.
JIMMY. And they respect you, in spite of themselves, for not telling.
AAMIR. I should have. Silence just makes bullying fester. They keep doing it 'cause nobody reports it.
JIMMY. Word is they have their sights on some other guy. His name is Jacob. Do you know him?
AAMIR. Nope.

JIMMY. He's new here. I've talked to him and am encouraging him to join our program. Hopefully, we will get so many members that being a bully will no longer be the cool thing to do.

AAMIR. These guys need some counseling.

*(**AMMIR** flips open **HIS** notebook.)*

JIMMY. Wha'cha writing?

AAMIR. A reminder to address the bullies in my speech. Did you know that Mrs. Hendrickson took some extra classes about counseling bullies? I met with her last week and she gave me some terrific ideas about our program. She's agreed to be our teacher mentor.

JIMMY. *(embarrassed)* Yeah, I know. I'm seeing her once a week.

AAMIR. You are? What for?

JIMMY. Remember, Aamir? Not so long ago *I* was the bully.

CURTAIN

PAN of POTATOES

CAST OF CHARACTERS

Mama - the gentle matriarch of thirteen children.

Ivah - fifteen, the tomboy and prankster.

Violet - fourteen and a budding beauty.

Lillas - seventeen and the 'big' sister.

LaVerne - twelve and the baby of the family.

Scene One

At Rise: The Guyer farmhouse. 1920. The kitchen. Morning.

(The four Guyer **SISTERS** *are setting the table, preparing breakfast and tea.* **MAMA** *is by the door putting on her hat and coat.)*

MAMA. Violet, don't let that mush burn. And save enough tea leaves for our supper tonight.
VIOLET. Yes, Mama.
MAMA. Ivah, you and LaVerne be sure to get your chores done while I'm in town. Lillas is in charge while I'm gone.

(The **GIRLS** *begin to talk and squabble.)*

MAMA. *(In a quiet voice.)* And girls....

*(**THEY** ignore her.)*

MAMA. GIRLS! *(They turn to her.)* I'm going into town and see Mr. Levine. Ask him for a little more credit until your father gets paid for that last load of lumber. I don't think that he'll let me shop on credit until the bill is paid down some but one can always hope. In the meantime, I've fried up the last of the
bacon, onion and spuds in the iron skillet. That's supper.

(The **GIRLS** *groan.)*

MAMA. I know. But, that's all there is until your father gets back tomorrow. *(Laughs.)* We'll pretend we live in a shoe, have so many children we don't know what to do.
IVAH. But, Mama, I'm so hungry!
MAMA. There's plenty of mush and...
LAVERNE. Mama, if the hens have produced can we have an egg this morning?
MAMA. Yes, of course. But I don't expect you to find anything. They should be about finished with molting. Hopefully we'll be seeing some eggs in a couple of days.
LAVERNE. *Yes,* Ma'am.
 LILLAS. That's okay, squirt. I'll help you look.
MAMA. Now, while I'm gone, you get your chores done, clean up the breakfast dishes, then you can play a game here at the table until I get back. Violet, is your bed made?

VIOLET. Yes...
> *(Simultaneously.)*
 IVAH. Is not.
VIOLET. Tattletale!
 IVAH. Beast!
MAMA. Girls!

 MAMA. What about the rest of you girls?
 IVAH. *(Smirking.)* Yes, Ma'am.
MAMA. Vi, get upstairs and make your bed. (MAMA reaches for the door handle.) And be good, all of you!

> *(SHE exits.)*

VIOLET. You've got a big mouth, you know that?
IVAH. You shouldn't lie to Mama.
VIOLET. It was a little white lie; Mama says that's okay.
IVAH. Did not.
VIOLET. Did too.

> *(THEY continue to squabble.)*

Scene Two

At Rise: Four hours later. The kitchen.

*(The **GIRLS** are sitting around the table playing Monopoly. **IVAH** is sitting in a   chair closest to the stove.)*

VIOLET. A hotel on Park Avenue. I'm winning!

LILLAS. Don't count your chickens, Vi, 'til they're hatched.

LAVERNE. *(Grumbling.)* Darn old hens, anyway! Why do they have to be molting right when we haven't any food in the house? And what is 'molting' anyway?

(LILLAS throws the dice.)

LILLAS. Damn! Jail, do not collect two hundred dollars.

LAVERNE. Swear word. I'm telllin' Mama.

LILLAS. No, you're not.

LAVERNE. Okay. What's molting, anyway.

VIOLET. They shed their feathers.

> *(**THEY** continue to play; meanwhile, **IVAH** is sneaking **HER** hand back and into the pan. **SHE** sneaks bites of the potatoes.)*

LAVERNE. Ugh! Then they're naked? Don't they get cold?

IVAH. Don't you know anything?   Yes! They're naked and they're so ugly your eye balls fall out.

LAVERNE. Really?

LILLAS. She's kidding you, squirt. They lose their old feathers and as soon as one is gone they start to grow a new one. But, it takes so much energy to do all that, they don't lay eggs.

> *(**THEY** continue to play and **IVAH**   continues to sneak bites of the potatoes.)*

VIOLET. LaVerne, pay attention! You landed on Boardwalk. You wanna buy a hotel or something?

LAVERNE. Lillas? What should I do? I don't have much money.

LILLAS. Go for it!

IVAH. *(Talking with her mouth full.)* Yeah, buy a bo-tel…

VIOLET. Ivah, what are you eating?

IVAH. *(Swallowing quickly.)* Nothing.

VIOLET. You are! What is it? I want some.

(LILLAS looks from IVAH's guilty face to the pan on the stove.)

LILLAS. Ivah! You've been eating our supper? *(crosses to the stove.)* You have! You've eaten almost all of the potatoes.

IVAH. Well, so what. I'm hungry!

VIOLET. But Mama said that's all we have.

IVAH. Oh, Fiddleydee! She'll get some credit and bring back supper fixin's.

VIOLET. What a selfish pig!

IVAH. Oh, shut up!

LAVERNE. You said, 'shut up'. Ivah, I'm telling.

IVAH. You shut up!

LILLAS. What are we going to tell Mama?

IVAH. NOTHING! You know our code, 'one for all and all for one'. You can't snitch me out.

Scene Three

At Rise: The Kitchen. An hour later.

(MAMA enters. SHE removes HER coat and hat off. HER hands are empty. The GIRLS sit at the table, silent.)

MAMA. Hello, girls. Sorry I was so long. That old skinflint, Levine, refused me credit. Told me my bill was too high and to 'bring him some money, then the store was mine'. Old badger. *(Silence.)* Well, never mind. Its bacon and spuds for us. Thank goodness we have that. Put your game away now and set the table. *(Silence. MAMA looks at them.)*What's happened? Who did what?
LILLAS. There's no bacon and spuds, Mama.

(MAMA crosses to the stove.)

MAMA. Of course there is. I fried them up this morning before I left. Plenty for everybody....*(looking in the pan.)*....Alright, what happened to supper? These potatoes didn't just sprout feet and run away.

(Silence. The GIRLS glare at IVAH.)

Oh, I see. 'One for all and all for one' is it? You thought I didn't know about your code of honor? *(Beat.)* You think anything in this house gets past your Mama? *(Silence.)* Well? I asked you girls a question. Are you going to tell me who did this? *(Silence.)*Well! That's fine. Humph! 'One for all,' is it? Well, good then *all* of you will be punished equally. Until the guilty party confesses to this greed, none of you are allowed to call me 'Mama'.
LAVERNE. But, Mama....
LILLAS. Mama....

(The GIRLS murmur with horror.)

 MAMA. And, you two, your punishment for calling me 'Mama' will be to clean out the chicken coop tomorrow morning. I don't want to hear another word until the person who did this comes to me. Now, get on up to bed without supper.
VIOLET. But, Mama, it's not even dark yet....
MAMA. One week of doing dishes for you young lady.

(THEY exit, muttering to each other.)

IVAH. Meeting at the outhouse.

VIOLET. *(Angry.)* Why should we?

LILLAS. Because we need to figure this out.

(THEY exit. And re-enter far down stage.)

LAVERNE. I hate the outhouse. It stinks.

VIOLET. Hush up..... Mama will hear us.

IVAH. Hold your nose.

LILLAS. Is that what you did while you ate our supper?

IVAH. Be quiet. I didn't know I had eaten so much. I thought I took just a couple of bites.

LILLAS. Well, you didn't. And now all of us are in trouble. I have never, in my life, been forbidden to call Mama, 'Mama'.

LAVERNE. I don't like this punishment. I want to call Mama by her name.

VIOLET. Ivah, you've got to tell Mama. This isn't fair. It's a terrible punishment. I'd rather cut my own switch and be licked with it than this.

IVAH. She's gonna be so mad at me. I can't tell her.

LILLAS. You've got to. It's not right that we are being punished when we didn't do anything wrong.

IVAH. I can't. Mama called the person who did this 'greedy'.

LILLAS. Yes, and that person is you!

VIOLET. I for one are not going to speak to you, loan you my hair ribbons, go places with you, or kill spiders for you, UNTIL YOU TELL MAMA THE TRUTH!

LAVERNE. Me too!

LILLAS. We have to vote. One for all and ...

IVAH. Yeah, yeah, we know, Lillas. Give it a rest.

LILLAS. *(Ignoring Ivah.)* All in favor of ignoring Ivah until she tells Mama, say 'Ay'.

VIOLET. 'Ay'.

LAVERNE. 'Ay'.

LILLAS. 'Ay'. 'Nays?'

IVAH. Nay.

VIOLET. Your vote doesn't count.

IVAH. This isn't fair. *(They have begun ignoring her.)* Can't we talk about this?

*(Silence. The **GIRLS** exit.)*

Scene Four

At Rise: Several days later. The kitchen.

(IVAH sits at the table alone doing homework. MAMA is at the sink.)

IVAH. Mama.....I mean, Mrs. Guyer.
MAMA. I'll let that slide, Ivah. What is it?
IVAH. I can't stand this. It's been almost a week and none of the girls will talk to me, Lillas and LaVerne wouldn't even let me help them clean out the chicken coop. Violet won't do anything with me.
MAMA. So....you're ready to tell me the truth?
IVAH. *(shocked.)* You knew? All this time, you knew!
MAMA. I know my girls. It was a pretty good guess who ate our supper.
IVAH. But, if you knew, why didn't you just say?
MAMA. Because then none of you would have learned anything.
IVAH. *(Rises and rushes to Mama)* Mama, I'm so sorry. I really didn't mean to eat the supper. I was sneaking a few bites and then suddenly it was mostly gone. Please, please forgive me. Please don't think
        I'm greedy.......*(she begins to cry.)...* even though it looks like I am. I'm so very sorry.
MAMA. Now, now. It's not the end of the world. Dry your tears. Did you learn anything, Ivah?
IVAH. Yes, Ma'am. Not to eat potatoes.
(MAMA can't help but laugh.)
MAMA. Yes, that too. But, I hope you also learned that you have to think of others sometimes. You can't be selfish. And above all else you must tell the truth and own up to your mistakes. Because no matter what you might do, I will always, always love you.
IVAH. Yes, Mama. *(Beat.) W*hat's my punishment going to be?
MAMA. I think you've been punished enough. Now, be a good girl, go out and get me a few carrots from the garden.

CURTAIN

The Run-Away

CAST OF CHARACTERS

Molly................a fifteen year old run-away

Rebecca..............Molly's mother, a single parent

Pete.................a pimp on the streets

Charlie..............a homeless woman

Various homeless people

Production Notes

None of the set suggestions, such as the bedroom, in the homeless camp, the street, need to be used. The dialogue and actors can create the scene.

'Jail bait' is a commonly used term for minor females that have an intimate relationship with someone over eighteen. In most states the adult can be charged and put in jail.

Charlie can hit Pete with anything handy in the room; a purse, a cane, a shopping bag. (Page 17)

This script affords the actor a chance to develop the skill of a one sided phone conversation.

Scene One

At Rise: Molly's bedroom. Early evening.

*(**REBECCA, MOLLY**'S mother sits on a stripped down bed waiting for **HER** daughter. The room has been stripped of everything **MOLLY** owns.)*

MOLLY. *(Off.)* Mom! I'm home! Mom? Where are you?
REBECCA. *(Shouts.)* I'm upstairs! Your room!

*(**MOLLY** enters, stops short when **SHE** sees **HER** bedroom and looks around in amazement.)*

MOLLY. *(Panic.) What did you do to my bedroom?*
REBECCA. *(Calmly.)* You're grounded for a month.
MOLLY. But, *what* did you *do* to my bedroom? Where's my TV…my laptop?
REBECCA. Until you obey my rules I've taken everything away. Give me your cell phone.
MOLLY. No.
REBECCA. Yes. Hand it over.

*(**MOLLY** wraps **HER** other hand protectively around **HER** phone.)*

MOLLY. I can't live without my phone. Why are you doing this to me?

*(**MOLLY** waves **HER** hands around, indicating the stripped room. As the hand holding the phone passes near **HER** mother, **REBECCA** snatches it away.)*

MOLLY. *(Lunges for the phone.)* Mother! Give it back!
REBECCA. You'll get it back in a month.
MOLLY. You are sooo mean! I hate you!
REBECCA. Until you learn the rules, starting with your being three hours late getting home today. You obvious don't need your phone because you didn't see a need to call me and let me know you wouldn't be home until….what?... *(Looking at her wrist watch)* six-thirty. Where have you been?

MOLLY. At school. I had detention.

REBECCA. And on top of everything else…you are lying to me.

MOLLY. *(Guiltily looks away.)* No, I'm not.

REBECCA. *(sighing.)* Molly, I called the school.

MOLLY. *(Shouts.)* You didn't! *(Guilty, she looks away. Beat.)* Okay! I went to the mall with some friends.

REBECCA. Another lie. You've been with Chad. Right?

MOLLY. *(Defiant.)* Yes! What have you got against him? You are sooo unfair. You don't even know him!

REBECCA. I know that he's nineteen and that you're fifteen. That's all I need to know.

MOLLY. Age means nothing. He doesn't care how old I am.

REBECCA. Oh, he'll care if it lands him in jail.

MOLLY. What are you talking about?

REBECCA. *(sighs.)* Molly, it's against the law for him to be 'dating' you…especially if you two are intimate.

MOLLY. *Moommm!* I am not discussing *that* with you!

REBECCA. I've always been very up front with you. I think you should wait to have sex. I've given you all the tools you need to make that decision. If you decide to have sex I've given you the tools to prevent pregnancy. But I have *always* hoped that you would wait.

(MOLLY will not look HER mother in the eye. REBECCA's eyes fill with tears.)

Oh, honey, please tell me that you are not having sex with that boy.

MOLLY. *(Yells.)* I am not talking to you about that! Now give me my stuff back. I want to check my email.

REBECCA. *(Rising.)* I told you, you are on punishment. No TV, no laptop, no phone, no email. When you begin to follow the rules you will slowly get your things back. First rule: you are not to see that boy anymore. Now wash up. I kept your dinner warm.

MOLLY. *You can't do this to me!*

REBECCA. Oh, yes, I can and I will. As long as you live in my house, eat my food, use my hot water, you will obey the rules.

MOLLY. *(Shouts.)* I hate you! I won't live here!

(REBECCA looks at HER daughter with compassion.)

REBECCA. Molls, don't you know I am just looking out for you…trying to keep you safe?

MOLLY. *(Turns to the door.)* I'm calling Dad. I'm telling. *(Sarcastic.)* That is, if you'll let me use *your* phone.

(MOLLY flounces out of the room. REBECCA calls after her.)

REBECCA. *(Calls after her.)* Be certain that you share how old Chad is, with your father.
MOLLY. *(Off.)* Shut up!

> *(An hour later. **MOLLY** comes into the living room, not looking at **HER** mother.)*

REBECCA. Did you eat?
MOLLY. Yes. *(Sarcastic.)* I appreciate you saving some of *your* food for me.
REBECCA. *(Ignores her daughter's tone.)* What did your Dad say?
MOLLY. He's so predictable. He said whatever you decided was probably fair. Then he had to go 'cause the baby was crying. It's disgusting, him having a baby with Tiffany at his age.
REBECCA. *(Choking back a laugh.)* Yes, forty is rather ancient.
MOLLY. Doesn't it bother you? Your husband has a kid with another woman?
REBECCA. He's not my husband anymore, Molls. But he is your father forever and he loves you.
MOLLY. I started the dishwasher and took the garbage out.
REBECCA. Thank you. For that, you get one hour of TV, in the living room.
MOLLY. *(Sarcastic.)* Gee, thanks!
REBECCA. Homework first.

> *(**MOLLY** gives **HER** mother a dirty look, rolls **HER** eyes and leaves to do **HER** homework. Moments later **MOLLY** yells down to **HER** mother.)*

MOLLY. *(Off.)* Mom! Where are my sheets? Where's my pillow? **REBECCA.** *(Yells back.)* You have to earn them.
MOLLY. *(Off.)* I can't believe you! You are such a witch!
REBECCA. *(Quietly, to herself.)* Yes, dear, I know.

Scene Two

At Rise: Late that night. MOLLY's bedroom.

*(**MOLLY** has stuffed **HER** long hair up under a baseball cap and **SHE** is wearing a coat. **SHE** is filling a backpack with her clothing.)*

MOLLY. *(Muttering to herself.)* I'll show you. I'll run away with Chad. You can't treat me like a prisoner. I have rights. I'll get a job and live with Chad.

*(Carrying **HER** backpack, **MOLLY** leaves the room and sneaks downstairs to the telephone. **SHE** dials Chad's number.)*

 MOLLY. *(Whispering.)* Chad, it's me. Sorry to call so late. *(pauses while Chad speaks.)* My mother is a total bitch…she took all my stuff. I'm being treated like a prisoner…I'm grounded for a month and…*(begins to cry.)*
I can't see you anymore. I'm running away. I want you to meet me…

*(**SHE** listens as Chad speaks.)*

MOLLY. what do you mean you can't?....I want us to be together. We can get a place and jobs….*(she listens as Chad interrupts.)*…what do you mean, 'jail bait'?...*(she listens)* …I don't care…I love you*!…(she listens again)*..you're breaking up with me? You can't. I'm running away…I want to be with you….*(the line goes dead. Chad has hung up.)*…hello? *Hello?*

*(Crying hard, **MOLLY** runs off.)*

*(Hours later, just before dawn **MOLLY** sits on the sidewalk, leaning against a wall. People come by and speak to **HER** but **SHE** doesn't look up and doesn't answer. A middle aged man walks up the street and stops when **HE** sees **MOLLY**.)*

PETE. Hey, pretty girl. What ya doin' sitting here all by yourself?

*(**MOLLY** doesn't look up; doesn't answer.)*

PETE. Ah, now, don't be shy. You got someplace to stay? You need a job? Tell ol' uncle Pete wha'cha need.
MOLLY. *(Mumbles, scared.)* I don't need anything. I don't know you. Go away.
PETE. Now, honey, don't be rude. Didn't your Mama teach ya to respect your elders.

MOLLY. She taught me not to speak the strangers.

(PETE laughs.)

PETE. It's cold out here. At least, let me buy you a cup of coffee.
MOLLY. No thank you.

*(Suddenly **PETE** takes **MOLLY** by the arm and hauls **HER** to **HER** feet.)*

PETE. Com'on. Coffee sounds good, don'cha think?
MOLLY. *(Tries to pull away.)* Let go. Leave me alone.
PETE. *(Keeps hold of her arm.)* Now, don't be mean to ol' Pete, honey. I can help you.
MOLLY. *(Struggles.)* I don't want your help. Let me go.

*(**PETE** begins to pull her down the street. **MOLLY** struggles in earnest now.)*

PETE. Come on. I got a real good job for a pretty little girl like you.
MOLLY. *(Panicked, she yells.)* Let me go! Help! Please! Help me!
PETE. *(Shakes her arm.)* Stop your yelling. Shut up!

*(**CHARLIE**, a homeless woman shuffles on and walks toward **THEM**.)*

CHARLIE. *(As she comes up to them.)* Hey! Pete! Let that girl go right now. What do you think your doin'?
PETE. Shut up, ya old hag. This ain't none of your business, Charlie.
CHARLIE. Well, I'm makin' it my business.
PETE. Yah? You and how many other bums?

*(**CHARLIE** takes a swing at **PETE** with **HER** purse. **MOLLY**, seeing **HER** opportunity to get free of **PETE** kicks **HIS** shins. **PETE** lets go of **MOLLY** to better avoid **CHARLIE**'s attack. **HE** gives up and tries to leave.)*

CHARLIE. *(Still hitting him.)* You're the bum, you *bum*! Go on, get outta here!

*(**PETE** starts to leave and **CHARLIE** continues to hit **HIM** and chases **HIM** down the block. **PETE** exits and **CHARLIE** returns to **MOLLY**.)*

MOLLY. *(Shaking.)* Thank you.
CHARLIE. That weren't nothin'. What's your name?

MOLLY. Molly.

CHARLIE. Just 'Molly'? No last name?

MOLLY. It's…ah…Smith…Molly Smith.

CHARLIE. Smith, huh? Okay. I'm Charlie. **MOLLY.** It's nice to meet you, Miss Charlie. Thank you for helping me.

CHARLIE. Well listen, *Molly Smith*, you gott'a stay clear of people like Pete. He's bad news and he'll hurt you if he gets a'hold of ya.

MOLLY. He wouldn't leave me alone. He was scary.

CHARLIE. Well you're safe now. But you see him comin'? You turn around and go the other way.

MOLLY. Yes, Ma'am.

CHARLIE. Ya hungry?

MOLLY. Yes, Ma'am.

CHARLIE. Ah now, don't 'Ma'am' me. I'm just plain old Charlie.

MOLLY. Yes, Ma….Charlie.

CHARLIE. Come on, there's a diner down the way that feeds some of us, out the back door.

(THEY chat as THEY do a slow cross.)

MOLLY. Can I ask you something?

CHARLIE. Sure. Don't know if I have the answers but you can ask.

MOLLY. Where do you stay…sleep?

CHARLIE. I got me a snug little camp down by the bridge. Why?

MOLLY. I need to find some place. Sleeping on the sidewalk last night was cold and scary.

CHARLIE. You got folks? A home, somewhere?

MOLLY. I don't want to talk about that.

CHARLIE. *(Throws her hands up.)* Okay, I understand. Some things are just too painful to talk about, right?

MOLLY. Yeah.

CHARLIE. Okay. So…what're ya gonna do?

MOLLY. Get a job…and then get an apartment.

CHARLIE. How old are you, kid?

MOLLY. Fifteen…almost sixteen.

CHARLIE. Fifteen, hmm? You know that nobody can hire you?

MOLLY. *(Starts to walk again.)* Really?

CHARLIE. Not 'till you're sixteen. When's your birthday?

MOLLY. Not for six months.

CHARLIE. Oh-oh, then you got a problem.

(As THEY exit.)

CHARLIE. Okay. Let's go get some grub and then I'll show you my place. You're welcome to stay while you figure things out.

Scene Three

At Rise: Charlie's camp. A week later.

(*CHARLIE* and *MOLLY* sit cross-legged on the ground. *THEY* both hold mugs of 'camp-coffee'.)

MOLLY. You were right, Charlie.
CHARLIE. Again?
MOLLY. I've been looking for a job for over a week now. Nobody will hire me…not even the golden arches… how flippin' hard is it to learn how to flip burgers?
CHARLIE. Yeah. They wouldn't hire me either and I'm way older than fifteen.
MOLLY. I don't know what I'm going to do. I'm almost out of money.
CHARLIE. Well…you're welcome to stay here.
MOLLY. And mooch off of you? Uh-uh. *(Beat.)*
I saw that Pete-guy when I was in town. He offered me a job. Said it paid good.
CHARLIE. And did he tell you what you'd have to do to get 'paid good.' **MOLLY.** Not really.
CHARLIE. Time for a little reality check, Molly. The job he's offering you is to go on 'dates' with strange men. Do I need to draw you a picture?
MOLLY. Ewww. That's gross.
CHARLIE. Exactly. And after Pete takes his cut, it don't pay so good. Stay away from that guy. He's trouble.
MOLLY. Okay.

(*THEY* sit in silence for a few beats.)

CHARLIE. You sure you don't want to call home, talk to your mother?
MOLLY. No! She'd never let me live it down if I went crawling back now.
CHARLIE. Do you think she's worried about you?
MOLLY. I guess.
CHARLIE. Look, I don't have kids, at least none that I've seen in more than ten years, but I can tell you your mother is worried crazy about you.
MOLLY. You think?
CHARLIE. She probably knows the score and is imagining someone like Pete getting their hands on you…she's probably frantic.

MOLLY. I can take care of myself.

CHARLIE. *(Dryly.)* Of course you can. *(Beat.)* But you don't see what I see on these streets, year after year. Hundreds of kids just like you disappear. One day I see 'em around and the next day they're gone. They get hooked on drugs, working for guys like Pete. They get beat up and worse. Lotta bodies found, right in this here river.

MOLLY. I don't want to talk about it anymore.

CHARLIE. Okay.

*(Silence for a beat. Then in spite of herself, **MOLLY** blurts out.)*

MOLLY. My mother is sooo mean!

CHARLIE. Beats ya, does she?

MOLLY. No…

CHARLIE. She a drunk?

MOLLY. No!

CHARLIE. A drug addict?

MOLLY. No!

CHARLIE. Starves ya?

MOLLY. No…but she's got rules…a million of them! Bam! She took away everything I own. She didn't even give my boyfriend a chance.

CHARLIE. Oh, well…that's just not fair.

MOLLY. Tell me 'bout it.

CHARLIE. The wicked witch of the West, for sure.

MOLLY. She's not like that all the time.

CHARLIE. Well, it's none of my business, of course, but I'll tell ya what I think anyway. Your mother wants what's best for you. And a nineteen year old guy is not what you need right now, Molly.

MOLLY. I guess.

CHARLIE. Did you lie to her about it?

MOLLY. Yes.

CHARLIE. Do you think lying is okay?

MOLLY. I guess not.

CHARLIE. So a person should have consequences when they lie?

MOLLY. Yeah.

CHARLIE. Your mother is just trying to teach you right from wrong…and lying is wrong and usually hurts *you* in the end.

MOLLY. That's what *she* says.

CHARLIE. A wise woman.

MOLLY. I kinda miss her.

CHARLIE. I think you should call her. Or I could call for you. Sort of smooth the way a little bit.

MOLLY. Really? You'd do that?

CHARLIE. Yeah. But you know, in order to earn her trust again, you'd have to take your punishment like a grown up and stop the lying.
MOLLY. I'll think about it.
CHARLIE. Fair enough.

*(**THEY** sit in silence for a beat.)*

CHARLIE. You ready to walk down to The Mission and get some chow?
MOLLY. I guess. It's not very good food, Charlie.
CHARLIE. You ever heard the saying, 'beggars can't be choosey'?
MOLLY. The salads are gross.
CHARLIE. I'll bet your Mom's a great cook, huh?
MOLLY. Yeah, she's pretty good, I guess.
CHARLIE. I had a mother once. She was the best cook in the world.
MOLLY. Mom makes awesome tacos.
CHARLIE. There ya go! Another fine reason to go home.

*(**MOLLY** grins at **CHARLIE**.)*

CHARLIE. *(Rising.)* Come on, let's go eat.
MOLLY. *(Rises.)* Okay. But, I'm not eating their salad.
CHARLIE. They got a phone we can use at The Mission, if you want.
MOLLY. Okay.

*(**THEY** exit.)*

Scene Four

At Rise: Later that same day. The Mission, a homeless shelter and soup   kitchen.

(CHARLIE and MOLLY are using the Mission's telephone. REBECCA, downstage left answers HER cell phone.)

REBECCA. *(Frowning, she looks at the caller ID.)* Hello?
CHARLIE. Mrs. Smith?
REBECCA. No…you must have the wrong num…
MOLLY. *(whispers in background.)* That's not my name…It's Sturdevant.

(CHARLIE frowns at MOLLY.)

 CHARLIE. Oh… *(Into the phone.)* Sorry…is this Mrs. Sturdevant.
REBECCA. Yes, who's calling?
CHARLIE. I'm Charlie…I'm a friend of Molly's.
REBECCA. Oh my God! Is she with you? Is she safe?
CHARLIE. Yes, she's here. But she wanted me to call you.
REBECCA. Can I speak to her?
CHARLIE. Yes, in just a minute.
REBECCA. And you're certain she's okay? She's not been hurt?
CHARLIE. No…no, she's fine.
REBECCA. Who are you again?
CHARLIE. My name is Charlie…Molly's been staying with me.
REBECCA. What's your address? I'll come right away.
CHARLIE. Well, that's a problem…I don't have an address.
REBECCA. *(Frantic.)* Please, Charlie, don't hurt her…I'll do anything you…she…wants.
CHARLIE. Look, I know you're scared. I don't want anything from you. And I think Molly should come home. But she's worried that you will punish her more and never let her live it down…that she done this dumb thing…in running away.
REBECCA. I won't!... punish her for running away. But she's got to understand that the grounding has to stick. She lied to me.
CHARLIE. I told her that.
REBECCA. *(Whispers.)* Thank you.

CHARLIE. I told her that you two need to sit down and talk about things. Will you do that?
REBECCA. *(Relieved.)* Yes, yes.
CHARLIE. Okay. Hold on….here's Molly.

*(**CHARLIE** hands the receiver to **MOLLY** and steps away, giving mother and daughter some privacy.)*

MOLLY. Mommy?
REBECCA. Molly! Are you all right?

*(At hearing **HER** mother's voice, **MOLLY** begins to cry.)*

MOLLY. Yes. I'm sorry, Mommy.
REBECCA. I'm sorry too, Molls.
MOLLY. Chad dumped me.
REBECCA. *(Chokes back a tearful laugh.)* Oh, honey, I'm sorry.
MOLLY. But you hated him.
REBECCA. I didn't hate *him*…I hated that he was too old for you.
MOLLY. That's what Charlie said.
REBECCA. Where have you been, Molly? How did you meet Charlie?
MOLLY. I met her the night,… well really, the morning after I left. I've been living with Charlie. She's got the coolest camp down by the river.

*(Realizing that **HER** daughter has been living with a homeless woman in a homeless camp, **REBECCA** starts to cry.)*

MOLLY. Mom, don't cry. I'm *okay*.
REBECCA. I know.
MOLLY. I know that it was wrong to lie to you about Chad. I want to earn your trust again. And Charlie says I have to take my punishment like a grown up.
REBECCA. *(Laughs.)* Your friend is a very wise woman. *(Beat.)* Will you come home? Will you let me come and get you?
MOLLY. Can we have your tacos tonight for dinner, Mom?

CURTAIN

THE 'D' WORD

CAST OF CHARACTERS

Richard - the father.

Polly - the mother.

Josh - the son.

Sarah - the daughter.

Scene One

At Rise: The living room of Richard and Polly' home. Evening.

(RICHARD and POLLY sit across the room from each other. JOSH enters, wearing an IPod and earplugs.)

JOSH. Whas' up?
RICHARD. Sit down, son.
JOSH. I got homework.
POLLY. Sit down, Josh.
(JOSH begrudgingly crosses and sits.)
POLLY. Where's your sister?
JOSH. How should I know?
RICHARD. Hey! Watch that tone with your mother.
JOSH. *(Mumbles.)* Whatever...
POLLY. Josh, a little respect would be nice...

(SARAH's entrance interrupts POLLY.)

SARAH. Hi Daddy. You're home early. What's going on?

(Crosses and sits next to HER father.)

RICHARD. Hi Baby. Your mother and I thought it was time for a family meeting.
JOSH. What'd I do now?
POLLY. Nothing. And please take the ear phones out and turn off your IPod.

(With a sigh, JOSH complies.)

SARAH. What's wrong? Why are you two being so polite?
RICHARD. Kids, your mother and I want you to know that no matter what happens, we love you. But sometimes...
 SARAH. *(Crying.)* No, no, no, I don't want to hear this.
POLLY. Sarah, honey, we need to talk to you both...

SARAH. NO! Daddy, please don't say it. Please, Josh and I will do better; won't we Josh. Please don't leave.

JOSH. Sar', what the heck are you blubbering about?

RICHARD. Sarah, calm down. I have to leave... you yourself asked me why your mother and I fight so much. I'll see you a bunch, I promise.

JOSH. Yeah. Like you're ever home now.

RICHARD. Honey, don't cry. You'll hardly know I'm gone.

JOSH. So nothing new there.

POLLY. Josh, you're not helping.

JOSH. So what? Am I supposed to be happy you two are getting a divorce?

SARAH. *(Horrified)* Divorce? Oh, no! Please, Daddy, don't. Please! *(She sobs.)*

POLLY. Sarah, honey, let Daddy and I tell you kids what's going to happen. That way you won't be so scared.

JOSH. I'm not scared.

POLLY. Your father and I have not been happy for some time now...

JOSH. *(Sarcastic.)* What else is new?

RICHARD. Josh, we need you to be respectful and a contributor. So cut the smart remarks.

POLLY. Anyway, as I was saying, your father and I think that a separation is a good idea. We're making everyone unhappy with all the arguments and harsh words.

SARAH. Please, please, can't you love each other? Can't you just get along?

RICHARD. It's not that easy, Princess. Sometimes adults, like your mother and I, still love each other but they're not in love anymore.

JOSH. *(A knowing look at his father.)* Or... they're in love with someone else now.

POLLY. That's enough, Josh.

SARAH. *(To Josh.)* What's that supposed to mean? *(To Richard.)* What's Josh talking about, Daddy?

RICHARD. Nothing, Baby. Josh doesn't know everything. In fact he knows shockingly little about life.

JOSH. *(Rises and exits.)* I am so outta here.

RICHARD. Josh! You come back here.

SARAH. *(In a tiny voice.)* What's going to happen now?

RICHARD. Well, I'm going to move out and...

SARAH. NO! Daddy, please...

POLLY. Sarah, just hear us out.

RICHARD. I'm going to move out. I've got an apartment in town. Just fifteen minutes away. You can come there whenever you want. I've got a bedroom for you and Josh and...

SARAH. *(Crying.)* How can this be happening? Susan said to me the other day how I was lucky that my parents were so solid. She hates that her Mom and Dad are split up. How can I face her or my other friends?

(SARAH rises, turns to her mother.)

You did this! You're driving him away! I HATE YOU!

(SARAH rushes out of the room.)

RICHARD. Sarah!
POLLY. *(Sarcastic.)* Well! That went well.
RICHARD. And I suppose that's my fault too.
POLLY. If the shoe fits...
RICHARD. Geez, Pol, give it a rest.
POLLY. How's Mary?
RICHARD. I'm not having this discussion with you again. Leave Mary out of it.
POLLY. That's pretty hard to do when she's the one breaking up my family. *(Beat.)* Don't you see what you're doing to your children? Don't you care, Richard?
RICHARD. Of course, I care!
POLLY. Then don't do it, Rich...we can work through this. We can get counseling...
RICHARD. Stop! *(Softer.)* Just stop, will you? We've talked about all of this before. I'm sorry but it's too late.
POLLY. Get out.
RICHARD. Pol...
POLLY. *(Angry.)* Get out, you selfish pig. How can you do this to your kids? Never mind about me. Don't you see how hurt and angry they are?
RICHARD. Of course I see...
 POLLY. *(Rising.)* Get out! Get out! Get out!
RICHARD. All right...I'm going...keep your voice down.

*(**RICHARD** rises and crosses the room.)*

Tell the kids 'bye'. I'll talk to them tomorrow.
POLLY. GET OUT!

*(**RICHARD** exits. **POLLY** sinks down onto the couch and buries her face in **HER** hands.)*

Scene Two

At Rise: The next afternoon. The living room.

*(**POLLY** is lying on the couch with a damp   towel over **HER** eyes. The front door slams. **JOSH** walks into the living room.)*

POLLY. Don't slam the door, please Josh.
JOSH. Sorry, Mom. *(Beat.)* What's wrong? Are you sick?
POLLY. No, sweetie. Just a headache.
JOSH. Is there anything to eat? The lunch at school was gross.
POLLY. *(Smiling.)* The kitchen is down the hall on your right.
JOSH. Very funny. I'm gonna get a snack before I start my homework. What time's dinner?
POLLY. Same ol', same ol'. Six-thirty just like always.
JOSH. Hey! Is Sarah home yet?
POLLY. Not yet. Today's Wednesday. Cheer leading practice after school.
JOSH. Mom, she wasn't at school today.
POLLY. *(Sits up.)*hat do you mean, not in school.
JOSH. Just what I said, she wasn't at school. At least, I didn't see her.
POLLY. Well, maybe you missed her.   **JOSH**. Much as I wish it wasn't true, I get to see her every day. Didn't today. It was kinda weird.
POLLY. Do you have your cell phone on you? *(Fishes it out of his pocket.)* Call her for me.
JOSH. *(Dials and listens.)*Straight to voice mail.
POLLY. Are you certain you didn't see her, Josh? *(**JOSH** shakes **HIS** head.)* Okay, buddy. She's probably in practice and turned her phone off. Go get your snack and start homework.
JOSH. Okay.

*(Shrugging **HE** exits.)*

Scene Three

At Rise: The living room. Three hours later.

(POLLY *and* **JOSH** *sit on the couch. The front door slams* **OFF**. **RICHARD** *rushes into the room.)*

RICHARD. Have you heard anything?

POLLY. No. I've called all her friends, nothing. The school confirmed that she was absent today.

RICHARD. What the devil happened? Why didn't the school call you and tell you she wasn't in school?

POLLY. School policy with honor roll kids is to call the parents on the second day of 'absent without a note'. They said they just assumed that she was out sick and I'd write her a note when she came back.

RICHARD. What'd she say to you this morning?

POLLY. I didn't see her before she left for school. She told me last night that she had an early committee meeting, before school, concerning the sophomore prom.

RICHARD. You didn't get up with the kids?

POLLY. I had a blinding headache and took something for it. I slept in.

RICHARD. Since when do my children get up and get themselves ready for school?

POLLY. Since over two years ago, Richard. They're not babies anymore. Oh, but wait! You're never at home to notice that they are teenagers now.

RICHARD. So my daughter skips school, disappears while my wife lays in bed with a headache.

POLLY. Don't make this my fault, Richard. I'm up every morning and more importantly, I'm here every evening. Can you say the same?

RICHARD. Give it a rest, Pol...

JOSH. *(Interrupts.)* Mom! Dad! Enough! Can you both give it a rest so we can find Sar'?

RICHARD. He's right. *(Beat.)* Have you called her phone? *(Beat.)* Yes, of course you have. Have you called the police?

POLLY. I wanted to wait until you got here. I was certain she would walk in the door.

RICHARD. I don't think we should wait. You call the police. I'll get in the car and start driving around. I've got my cell; call me if you hear anything.

(RICHARD *rises and starts to exit.)*

JOSH. Dad, can I come with you? I know some places where she and her friends hang.

(RICHARD looks at POLLY and SHE nods.)

RICHARD. Sure, son. Be glad to have you with me.

(THEY exit. POLLY dials HER phone.)

Scene Four

At Rise: Two days later. The living room.

(RICHARD and POLLY sit together on the sofa. JOSH sits in a chair nearby.)

POLLY. This has got to be a parent's worst nightmare. To see an 'Amber Alert' with *your* child's name. My God, Richard, what if they don't find her? I can't stand it! I'll die.
RICHARD. Easy, Baby. They'll find her. It's going to be okay.
JOSH. *(Scared.)* Dad...

(POLLY's cell phone rings. SHE grabs it off the coffee table.)

POLLY. HELLO! Sarah, is that you? *(Beat.)* Oh, Hello, Mrs. McClury. *(Covers the phone with her hand.)*... It's Carolyn's mother. *(Back to the phone.)* I really can't talk now. I have to leave the phone line open for Sarah….or the police. Yes. *(Listens for several beats.)* WHAT!? She's there?...Oh, my God, she's there with you*?...(Listens.)* Is she all right*?* Oh, thank you! Yes, yes, we'll wait right here....Yes, I understand. No, no, that's perfectly fine. *(Beat.)* Please, Mrs. McClury, will you tell her that she's not in trouble. Tell her to just, please, come home. Yes, yes. See you in ten minutes. Thank you! Bye.
POLLY. The whole time. Carolyn was hiding her in their basement. Mrs. McClury said she came home early from work today and thought she heard water running. She went down in the basement to see and found Sarah in the shower. She called us right away but not before she gave Sarah a good talking to. She tried to apologize for that. *(Laughing with relief.)* It saves me from giving her a lecture. Said she grounded Carolyn for a month.
 JOSH. That's so lame. What's Sarah's punishment?
RICHARD. We'll decide later, Josh. When she gets here I want you to go to your room.
JOSH. Why?
      RICHARD. Because I said so. First Mom and I need to talk to her alone. Then you can come back down. Deal?
JOSH. Whatever.
RICHARD. Thank you.

*(The door bell rings **OFF. RICHARD** and   **POLLY** jump up. As **THEY** cross to the door, **JOSH** exits.)*

POLLY. *(OFF.)* Sarah! Baby, are you all right?
 MRS. McCLURY. *(OFF.)* I'm so sorry about this.

RICHARD. *(OFF.)* Thanks, Mrs. McClury, Carolyn. Talk to you soon. Bye.

*(**ALL** three enter the living room. **THEY** sit on the sofa.)*

SARAH. Are you guys really mad at me?

RICHARD. No, Princess, we were just very worried.

POLLY. I'm not angry with you, Sar', but don't you ever scare me like that again.

SARAH. I'm sorry, Mom.

POLLY. What possessed you to run away like that?

SARAH. *(Crying.)* I couldn't stand it...Daddy's leaving...it hurts so much...

POLLY. Do you know what could have happened to you? Thank God Carolyn hid you in their basement. When I think what...

RICHARD. But nothing bad happened, Pol. Let's leave it at that.

SARAH. What's my punishment?

POLLY. Your Dad and I will let you know. Tomorrow.

SARAH. Are you going to stay, Daddy?

RICHARD. Princess. I can't. Your running away didn't 'fix' anything. I know this is tough on you kids. I'm sorry about that. Your Mom and I love you so much and we're going to do everything possible to make this easier for you.

POLLY. Let me call Josh.

*(**POLLY** rises and exits.)*

POLLY *(OFF.)* Josh. Come down, please.

*(**SARAH** returns. **JOSH** enters the room and sits.)*

POLLY. Okay, family meeting. Richard, would you tell Josh what you were saying to Sarah.

RICHARD. Listen, buddy. I know that this is tough. And your Mom and I are really sorry that we're hurting you. We'll never stop loving both of you, you know that right? I'll still be your Dad even though I won't be living here. I'll see you anytime you want.
You can come to my apartment whenever you want, right, Polly?

POLLY. Absolutely.

RICHARD. We'll have sleepovers.

JOSH. No way.

RICHARD. Order pizza with pineapple, and you can watch anything you want on TV for however long you want.

POLLY. I don't think we'll go quite that far. But, we'll see. The important thing to remember and know with all your heart is you two didn't do anything wrong. Your Dad and I screwed it up. And even though our living arrangements are going to change, it absolutely,   positively, does not change how much we love you.

 RICHARD. Ditto for me.

SARAH. You're not going to leave us, like forever, right Daddy?

JOSH. Geez, Sar', you are so lame.

RICHARD. I would never leave you two guys. Your my kids, and… *(Looks at his daughter.)* You're my Princess. *(Beat.)* And, Josh...

JOSH. Yeah?

RICHARD. As the oldest, I expect you to watch over your sister and your Mom when I'm not here. Understand?

JOSH. Yeah, I guess.

RICHARD. And you both gotta promise to come and talk to one of us if you feel scared or worried. Got it, Josh?

JOSH. Got it, Dad.

RICHARD. Princess? You promise you'll come to one of us?

SARAH. I promise.

POLLY. Okay. Who wants hamburgers?

(SARAH and JOSH jump up and exit for the kitchen.)

Can you stay, Richard?

RICHARD. *(Rising.)* For your hamburgers? Try to keep me away.

(As THEY exit, RICHARD puts a casual arm across POLLY's   shoulders.)

CURTAIN

THE POSTCARD

CAST OF CHARACTERS

Betsy - Mid-forties. The mother of Elizabeth.

Elizabeth - Early-twenties, she is the bride-to-be.

Joe - Elizabeth's fiancée. He is in his late twenties.

Scene One

At Rise: A living room.

(BETSY sits with a cup of tea, addressing envelopes. She is humming the wedding march under her breath. ELIZABETH, her daughter, enters, her arms full of magazines, catalogs, and mail.)

ELIZABETH. Mother!
BETSY. Here, darling.

(ELIZABETH whirls around and crosses to her mother, waving the mail.)

ELIZABETH. More wedding catalogs, Mom.   Wanna look at them now?
BETSY. Later, darling. You'd better get showered. Joe will be here in less than an hour.
ELIZABETH. *(Grabs her mother's wrist to check the time.)* Holy Smokes!   Where did the time go? We were having such fun with the menu for the reception, I had no idea it was so late.

(SHE begins to run from the room.)

See you in a minute, Mom.
BETSY. Lizzy-bug...
ELIZABETH. *(Stops and turns.)* Yes?
BETSY. The mail's going to get wet.

(Looking baffled SHE glances down at the mail in HER hands. SHE begins to laugh. SHE rushes back and dumps all the mail into her mother's lap.)

ELIZABETH. Oh! Right. *(Exits.)* Back soon.
BETSY. *(Mutters.)* Where in the world did I get a child like that?

(Still humming the wedding march and going through the various   envelopes, BETSY comes to a postcard with a colorful bunch of flowers on the back. SHE turns the postcard over.)

BETSY. What? why is Lizzy sending me a postcard? *(reading aloud.)* 'Dear Mom...I hope you don't mind me calling you that. I don't know what to say...or where to begin, but I had to write you, now that I have found you.'

*(**BETSY** lays her head back on the chair. She continues to read.)*

BETSY. 'Please, please don't rip this up until you read it all. I so want to meet you, see you. I have ever since I was old enough to know what 'adopted' meant. Please call me at the number below...... I'll be waiting. Love, Sally.'

*(**BETSY** stares at the postcard. The doorbell sounds. Rising and crossing to the door, **SHE** opens it to find **JOE**, Elizabeth's fiancée.)*

BETSY. Joe! *(Hugs him.)*   How many times do I have to tell you? This is your home, so just walk right in.
JOE. *(Laughing.)*   I know, Betsy, I know.   My Mom's training keeps getting in the way.
BETSY. *(Crosses to her chair and sits.)* So after the wedding my new son is going to ring the doorbell like a...   *(Laughs.)* ... a vacuum salesman.
 JOE. Who knows? If the market keeps going the way it has, I just might sell you a vacuum...
ELIZABETH. *(Off.)* Mom!
BETSY. Darling....Joe's here.
ELIZABETH. *(Off.)* Hi, my love...
JOE. Hi, 'Lizzy-bug'!
ELIZABETH. Don't. Call. Me. That.   See what you've created Mom?
BETSY. *(Not sorry at all.)*   Sorry, darling.
ELIZABETH. *(Off.)* Be out in a jiffy. Mom, show Joe the menu.
JOE. Oh, no, please.   No more. I don't wanna see the menu.
BETSY. *(Laughing.)* Don't worry, I won't. There are some things that the groom just doesn't need to know.
JOE. Thank you! You're an angel of a mother-in-law. How's she doing?
BETSY. She's like a small, benign hurricane. And I've never seen her happier. You're good for her, Joe. So calm and unflappable. Thank you for that.
JOE. I promise I will remain so...if I don't have to see the menu for the reception.
BETSY. It's a deal. When Lizzy asks you what you think, tell her you love it.

*(A small silence; **BETSY** gazes out the window. **JOE** watches her.)*

JOE. How's the mother of the bride today? *(She does not answer.)* Earth calling Mom.

*(**BETSY** jumps and focuses on **JOE**.)*

BETSY. Oh, sorry, dear. What were you saying?
JOE. You okay?
BETSY. Yes, certainly. Never better...

(ELIZABETH whirls into the room and SHE throws HERSELF into his arms.)

ELIZABETH. Joey! I've missed you so much.

JOE. It's been six hours, Lizzy.

ELIZABETH. That long?

BETSY. Children, please sit down. I would like to discuss something with you...

ELIZABETH. What is it, Mom? What's wrong?

BETSY. I got a letter in the mail...well, not a letter, really. A postcard...

JOE. Why don't you two girls talk and I'll go in the kitchen and find myself a beer. You ladies want more tea?

BETSY. I'd like you to stay, please, Joe. Ever since Lizzy's father died, I find myself relying more and more on you.

ELIZABETH. Of course, you'll stay, Joey. You're part of our family... is it something to do with the wedding? I knew everything was going too smoothly...all my friends had the most terrible time planning their weddings...their mothers turned into monsters...the flowers didn't arrive on time...one bridesmaid gained a bunch of weight and couldn't get into her dress...why, Mary Jo's church was double booked!...Can you imagine?

BETSY. Elizabeth.

ELIZABETH. Sorry Mom. What is it?

BETSY. Now listen carefully, Lizzy, to what I am about to tell you. It changes nothing...NOTHING...you are still my best girl and I love you very much...

ELIZABETH. *(Tears fill her eyes.)* Oh my God!   You've got cancer.   I knew things were too good to be true. Daddy last year and now this...

BETSY. Darling...no...no...I'm fine. I'm not sick. It's just that I got this postcard and now I have to tell you something...

ELIZABETH. Oh, Mommy, you scared me.   *(Beat.)* What's a dumb old postcard got to do with anything?

JOE. Lizzy, your Mom is trying to tell us. Maybe if you listen for a few, very short minutes, we'll understand.

ELIZABETH. Of course! How silly. My mouth is always running...I can't seem to help it.

BETSY. As you know, Lizzy, I started at the University when I was seventeen. In my sophomore year, I met a senior and fell madly in love.

ELIZABETH. Daddy?

BETSY. No dear. This was years before I met Dad. Anyway, six months later I found out that I was pregnant. I went to my boyfriend with the news. I thought he'd be happy about a baby. He would graduate before it was born and I would continue with my classes until I got further along. We'd be married and live happily ever after. *(A derisive laugh.)* My goodness, I couldn't have been more wrong. He disappeared from my life. If we happened to meet on campus, he didn't know me. It was so embarrassing. So, I transferred and finished the year out. When the baby was born, I gave it up for adoption.

ELIZABETH. Oh Mommy....

JOE. That was pretty brave of you, Mom.

BETSY. I don't know. Sometimes I think it was pretty cowardly of me. I was on full scholarship and still had to work two jobs just to get by. How could I support a baby too?

ELIZABETH. But, I don't see what this has got to do with my wedding....

JOE. I think I do. *(Beat.)* Let your Mom tell us the rest, Lizzy.

BETSY. In the mail...today... *(holds it up.)* I got this postcard.. ...from *her*.

ELIZABETH. From who? Oh! 'H*er*'? You mean you had another daughter?

BETSY. Yes, dear. A daughter, your sister, Sally...

ELIZABETH . NO! Absolutely not! You're my mother...(Begins to cry.)....you're not hers!

(BETSY rises and crosses to ELIZABETH. SHE sits on the other side of her.)

BETSY. Of course I'm your mother, Lizzy-bug. I love you best, always. You're my own sweet girl...

ELIZABETH. What does she want?

BETSY. She wants us to meet. You may read the note if you wish.

ELIZABETH . *(Inconsolable.)* No!...I don't want you to meet her. She's nothing to us....she's not your daughter, I AM! How could you?

JOE. Easy, honey.

BETSY. How could I what, Lizzy?

ELIZABETH. Everything! *(Hysterical.)* Get pregnant! Give your baby away! Not tell me! *(Beat.)* Why didn't you tell me? We tell each other everything. You said so...

BETSY. I didn't tell you because it was so long ago. I never imagined that it would touch our lives. I knew that she had gone to good people who would take care of her and love her...

ELIZABETH. Stop calling her, 'her'. She's got a name. Sally.

BETSY. Yes...Sally.

ELIZABETH. She's real. *(Beat.)* Oh, my God, she's real.

JOE. What're you going to do, Mom?

BETSY. I don't know. What do you want me to do, baby?

ELIZABETH. *(SHE rises, crosses to the door.)* It's not up to me, it's not! You have to decide. She seems to think that she's your daughter...but whatever you do... don't tell me...I don't want to know...she's not part of my life.

(ELIZABETH exits.)

BETSY. *(Sighing.)* Go to her, Joe. She needs you.

JOE. It's going to be okay, Mom. Just let Elizabeth get used to the idea...the stress of the wedding...It's been a huge shock for everyone...especially you. *(Beat.)* I'd better go and find her.

BETSY. Yes, darling...*(As he crosses.)* and Joe?

JOE. Yes.

BETSY. Thank you, my boy.

JOE. Don't thank me. It's my job as your favorite son-in-law. Don't worry, okay Mom?

*(**JOE** exits. **BETSY** sits back down in her chair. Almost immediately, **JOE** and **ELIZABETH** come back into the room. **ELIZABETH**'s head is down. **THEY** walk to the front door.)*

JOE. Mom, we're going for a ride, maybe catch a movie. We won't be late. See you later.
BETSY. All right, my darlings. Be careful. Have fun.

*(**BETSY** sits in the chair. **SHE** picks up the postcard and reads it again. **SHE** looks at the phone. **SHE** rises and crosses to the phone, refers to the postcard and then dials.)*

BETSY. Hello...yes, I'd like to speak to Sally, please. This is Betsy Graves calling...Oh! It's you... Sally...this is your...mother.

CURTAIN

Cyber-Hate

Production Notes

1) The blocking is with Rachel (stage right) and Cathy (stage left) sitting with their backs to each other and profiles to the audience. Josh is upstage center, sitting with his back to the audience.
2) The scene can be study hall, their individual bedrooms, or a cyber café hang out, depending upon the dialogue and the director.
3) This blocking reflects the struggle for control between the girls. Josh is a non-entity, thus his back is to the audience. He is the 'possession' that the girls are fighting about, as they are both dating Josh.
4) All three type as they speak their lines.
5) When other friends chat with the characters, the actors read both parts (at their computers) or director could opt for a voice-over.
6) If the director wishes to increase the cast size, the friends who chat with the girls on-line could be present on stage.
7) See glossary for abbreviations on the Internet and urban slang.
8) Scene 5: If the director opts for smaller cast, Bethany's lines can be cut.

Author's Notes

This script is based on a true story about cyber-bulling which ended in one of the girls stabbing her rival to death, over a boy.

Despite the potential damage of cyber bullying, it is alarmingly common among adolescents and teens. According to Cyber bullying statistics from the i-SAFE foundation:
www.isafe.org/about?ch=op&sub_id=media_cyber_bullying

Over half of adolescents and teens have been bullied online, and about the same number have engaged in cyber bullying.
More than 1 in 3 young people have experienced cyber threats online.
Over 25 percent of adolescents and teens have been bullied repeatedly through their cell phones or the Internet.
Well over half of young people do not tell their parents when cyber bullying occurs.

CAST OF CHARACTERS

Rachel - a teenage girl and a cyber-bully

Joshua - the boy both girls are fighting over

Cathy - a teenage girl, a victim of cyber-bullying

Bethany (optional) - A friend of Rachel's

River (optional) - Cathy's best friend

Scene One

At Rise: After school. Late afternoon.

(**RACHEL** *and* **CATHY** *sit at tables working on* **THEIR** *laptops, with* **THEIR** *backs to each other.* **JOSH** *sits at a table, center upstage,   typing on* **HIS** *laptop.*)

RACHEL. *(typing and reading aloud)* Hi.
JOSH. *(answering)* Hi Rach', wha'cha doing?
RACHEL. Homework. You?
JOSH. The same. Algebra is so lame. I'm never going to get it.
RACHEL. I could help you, if you want.
JOSH. Could you? That would be great. If only you could take my test for me too. lol.

(A text dings in. It's **CATHY** *messaging* **JOSH**.*)*

JOSH. *(typing)* Hold on, Rach….I've got a text..
RACHEL. Okay.
JOSH. BRB.

(**RACHEL** *continues to sit and stare at* **HER** *screen.*)

JOSH. *(reading, he begins to type)* Hi, Cathy.
CATHY. Hi, Josh. It's Friday, yeah!
JOSH. Do you have much HW for the weekend?
CATHY. Just a 10 page essay for English. You?
JOSH. Same.
CATHY. Are you going down to the Surf and Slurp tomorrow?
JOSH. *(flirting)* I could be….you?
CATHY. *(flirting)* Why do you think I'm asking?

(Tired of waiting, **RACHEL** *has sent an email and* **JOSH**'s *laptop chimes.*)

JOSH. Just a sec, Cathy, got an email. BRB.
CATHY. Don't be long.
JOSH. Sorry 'bout that, Rach. It was Cathy texting me.
RACHEL. What did *she* want?
JOSH. Just to chat.
RACHEL. She knows we're dating, right?

JOSH. I don't know if she does. But, we're not hanging out exclusively; you know that, right?

RACHEL. *(disappointed)* Of course I know.

JOSH. I better go…get this homework banged out so my weekend is free.

RACHEL. Will I see you tomorrow?

JOSH. Sure. I'll call you. Bye.

RACHEL. Bye.

JOSH. *(types)* You still there?

CATHY. Yes. But, I was about to give up. If you're busy right now, we can talk later. No prob'.

JOSH. No, no! I'm not busy.

CATHY. OK. *(beat)* You were saying about tomorrow?

JOSH. Want to go to the Drip with me?

CATHY. I'd love to. What time?

JOSH. Eleven? I like my beauty sleep on Saturdays.

CATHY. Like you need it. LOL Eleven is good.

JOSH. Okay. See ya there.

CATHY. Bye.

JOSH. Later.

Scene Two

At Rise: Saturday afternoon.

(RACHEL *sits at* **HER** *laptop, typing. An open text book to the side.* **CATHY** *sits at* **HER** *laptop, facing out,* **SHE** *is reading a book.* **JOSH**'s *chair is empty. The chime of an email chimes on* **RACHEL**'s *laptop.)*

RACHEL. *(typing)* Hey, Bethany. What are you doing?
BETHANY. *(typing, reading aloud)* Hey, Rachel, nothing much. You'll never guess who I saw at the Surf N' Slurp this morning!
RACHEL. *(typing)* You know I hate guessing games. Who?
BETHANY. *(typing) Cathy!*
RACHEL. So?
BETHANY. So….it's *who* she was with that's ridiculous!
RACHEL. *(typing)* Just spit it out, Bethany. Who??
BETHANY. Josh!
RACHEL. *(typing furiously) My* Josh??
BETHANY. That's the one.
RACHEL. Together? You're sure?
BETHANY. Oh, I'm sure, all right. They were holding hands.
RACHEL. *What!!?*
BETHANY. Yep.
RACHEL. That slut! She *knows* Josh and I are dating!
BETHANY. I knooww, right? *(Beat)* But, Rach', you're not exclusive-like, are you?
RACHEL. Nooo…not yet, but we will be.
BETHANY. So….?
RACHEL. So would you do this if you knew Josh and I were hanging out…almost exclusive?
BETHANY. No, but I'm your friend. That's why I told you that I saw them.
RACHEL. That b-yatch! I'll get her for this.
BETHANY. That's for sure…going after someone else's boyfriend is just wrong.
RACHEL. She'll be sorry.
BETHANY. What're you gonna do?
RACHEL. Start with Facebook, what else?
BETHANY. Oooo…I can't wait.
RACHEL. No one will like her when I'm finished. Nobody likes a boyfriend stealer. Let me go…I've got some comments I want to post on my page.
BETHANY. Okay, c u later.

RACHEL. Talk at you soon. Bye.

(**RACHEL** *signs off and immediately signs on to Facebook.*)

RACHEL. *(typing and reading aloud)* I'll tell you what's on my mind!   What blond slut was seen with my boyfriend, today, at the Drip Café? She's too ugly to get her own boyfriend…she has to go after someone else's. What a tool! Girls! Watch out…you could be next. This ho will do anything, and I mean *anything,* to get your man.

(**RACHEL** *gloats as* **SHE** *stares at the screen.* **CATHY**'s *laptop dings.* **SHE** *puts down the book* **SHE** *was reading and turns to* **HER** *laptop. SHE types.*)

VOICE *(Off.)* You have five Facebook notifications.
CATHY. *(reading the latest posting, silently)* Oh!
How dare she? What a jealous, spiteful girl!
(reading some of the other comments) 'What's with this thing with Josh?' *and* 'Don't mess with Rachel's man, lol' *and* 'What blond slut is she talking about? Fill me in.'

(**CATHY** *signs off Facebook and immediately begins a text to* **RACHEL.**)

CATHY. *(typing and reading aloud)* Who's a slut? How dare you? Your so-called boyfriend asked *me* out. Last time I looked it was a free country. Besides, you and Josh are not exclusive!
RACHEL. *(typing) You're the slut!* Only sluts go after someone else's boyfriend. You better keep your hands off Josh. He belongs to *me!* If you don't, you better watch your back, you ugly tool. I'll get you and then you'll be sorry you ever messed with me!

(**RACHEL** *stabs at the keys.* **CATHY** *begins to type a response but* **RACHEL** *has signed off.)*

CATHY. OMG! What a mean girl…I didn't 'go after', quote, unquote, her boyfriend. Does she think I'm afraid of her?

Scene Three

At Rise: A week later.

(CATHY sits at her laptop. Rachel and Josh's chairs are empty. CATHY is on line with HER best friend, RIVER. CATHY reads RIVER's text.)

RIVER. I can't believe what Rachel is saying about you, Cath'.
CATHY. *(typing)* I knooww! She is such a bully.

(SHE hits enter on the keyboard and waits for RIVER's reply.)

RIVER. What are you gonna do?
CATHY. I don't know, River. Josh keeps asking me out. He says to ignore Rachael. That they were never exclusive and he was always honest with her about that.

(While the GIRLS chat, RACHEL enters and sits in HER chair. SHE begins to type.)

RIVER. I was bullied in middle school. It was no fun!
CATHY. You? Really?

(CATHY's laptop chimes. SHE looks at the sender.)

CATHY. OMG, River, I'm getting an email from Rachel.
RIVER. Don't answer it, Cath'.
CATHY. I have to….don't go anywhere, I'll be right back.

(CATHY opens the email from RACHEL.)

CATHY. *(typing)* What do you want, Rachel?
RACHEL. *(typing)* I'm warning you for the last time, slut. You better stop seeing Josh.
CATHY. Or what, Rachel? You should talk to your boyfriend, not me.
RACHEL. That's right! 'My boyfriend'! And if you don't butt out, I'll make you sorrier than you can imagine. You're an ugly ho and everybody knows it.
Everyone says you're having sex with Josh to keep him.
CATHY. *(typing furiously)* I am not! That's a lie!
RACHEL. I'll hurt you, do you hear me? You can't have him. I WILL HURT YOU!

*(**CATHY** sits back from **HER** computer as if a snake struck out at **HER**. **SHE** signs off **CATHY** switches back to **RIVER**.)*

CATHY. You there, River?
RIVER. Yes! What did she want?
CATHY. More name calling. She said she knew I was having sex with Josh.
RIVER. I know. I read that on Facebook. *(beat)* Are you?
CATHY. NO!
RIVER. I didn't think so. We have a BFF pack, right? Definitely no sex with a boy until we're at least engaged, right?
CATHY. *(sighing)* Right.
RIVER. What else did she say?
CATHY. Oh, nothing rational. Rachel just went off the deep end. Made some silly threats.
RIVER. Like?
CATHY. She said, 'I'll hurt you'.
RIVER. Really?
CATHY. Yeah. How weird is that?
RIVER. Ridiculous weird.
CATHY. I don't want to talk about her anymore. Tell me about middle school.
RIVER. Oh that. I got my share of bullying…actually more than my share. All through middle school.
CATHY. Really? I can hardly believe it. You're so popular now. What happened?
RIVER. Oh, the usual, you know. Called me names, told lies about me. It was all over Facebook.
CATHY. Like what?
RIVER. Called me 'Injun', 'squaw', 'half-breed' …they said all Indians steal and lie.
CATHY. Oh, River, that's terrible.
RIVER. The worst part was that my Mom blocked me from going on Facebook for almost a year.
CATHY. Wow.
RIVER. Yeah, my grades slipped and she blamed it on the bullying on Facebook. Of course, she was right, I was pretty depressed.
CATHY. How did you stop it? I feel like this is never going to end.
RIVER. Much to my horror, my Mom got in touch with the bullies' parents and explained to them that cyber bullying and threats are against the law and that their kids, and maybe even their parents, could get arrested.
CATHY. OMG! Did you just die of embarrassment?
RIVER. You have no idea! But one day the bullying just stopped….like it had never happened.
CATHY. I can't believe it…everyone loves you at school. You're so pretty and you volunteer for just about everything. All the girls copy what you wear.
RIVER. Hang in there, Cath', it's got to end.
CATHY. I know….but when?
RIVER. Do your parents know?

CATHY. NO! They'd have a cow if they knew.

RIVER. I think you should tell them, Cath', especially after what Rachel said to you today.

CATHY. Uh-Uh. They hate social networking. If it was up to them they wouldn't let me do it at all. If they find out about this they'll forbid me to go on-line ever. And they would probably make certain I didn't see Josh anymore.

RIVER. Are you serious about him?

CATHY. I really like him. He's fun and funny.

RIVER. You know, don't you, that he is still seeing Rachel.

CATHY. That's up to him. None of my business.

RIVER. My, aren't we all grown up. Aren't you just a little jealous?

CATHY. No, why should I be? We're not exclusive.

RIVER. Well, Rachel should take a page from your book, girlfriend.

Scene Four

At Rise: A week later. Evening.

(RACHEL *sits at her laptop, stage left.* **CATHY** *is typing at* **HER** *laptop.* **JOSH** *sits upstage at* **HIS** *laptop, reading an email.)*

RACHEL. *(typing and reading aloud)* Hi Josh, honey.
JOSH. *(typing)* Hey, Rach, where'd you disappear to this afternoon?
RACHEL. I saw you walking down the hall with Cathy. *(sarcastic)* I didn't want to interrupt anything.
JOSH. Oh.
RACHEL. Why do you need to date her, Josh?
JOSH. I like her.
RACHEL. Oh. *(beat)* Better than you like me?
JOSH. Not necessarily. But there isn't as much drama with her.
RACHEL. And that's a good thing?
JOSH. Yes. *(beat. there's an IM chime)* Hold on, I'm getting a message. BRB.

(JOSH *switches over to the IM while* **RACHEL** *types frantically.* **HE**'s *already gone so* **HE** *doesn't see what* **RACHEL** *has typed.)*

RACHEL. *(typing; banging the keys)* Josh! If that's your ho girlfriend, you better not answer her!
JOSH. *(typing)* Hi Cath'. I am so happy to hear from you. I miss you.
CATHY. *(typing)* I miss you too. Sorry I had to rush home this afternoon.
JOSH. Wha'd you have to do?
CATHY. Mom calls it 'spring cleaning' but it's really 'Cathy the slave' time. lol. I had to clean every cupboard in the kitchen!
JOSH. LOL, poor kid.
CATHY. Tell me about it.
JOSH. Listen, I was just on line with Rachel. Can I text you when I get finished?
CATHY. Sure.
JOSH. Cathy, listen, I want you to know. I'm going to break up with her.
CATHY. You are?
JOSH. All this stuff she's been writing on Facebook; it's disgusting. I don't want to hang out with someone like that.
CATHY. Well, we don't know for sure it's her, Josh.
JOSH. Oh, it's her all right. *(beat)* And I want to ask you something.
CATHY. What?

JOSH. I want to be exclusive with you. What do you think?

CATHY. I want that too, Josh. But I don't want Rachel to get hurt. She really, *really* likes you.

JOSH. I'll take care of her. *(beat)* So, does that mean we're exclusive?

CATHY. Not until you tell Rachel.

JOSH. Sick. I'll tell her right now. I'll text you when I'm done.

CATHY. Okay. Later.

JOSH. Bye.

> *(CATHY rises and exits. **JOSH** clicks back to **HIS** chat with **RACHEL**. The first thing **HE** sees is the IM that **RACHEL** sent, a few minutes ago, as **HE** switched over to **CATHY**. Sighing, **HE** switches off **HIS** laptop and picks up **HIS** cell phone; speed dials **RACHEL**'s cell. **RACHEL's** cell phone rings.)*

JOSH. Rachel? It's me.

RACHEL. *(hurt and angry)* Josh, I thought you forgot about me. Who was that you were talking to for so long?

JOSH. Never mind about that. *(sighs)* Rachel, that was an ugly thing you wrote before.

RACHEL. I don't care. I don't see why you have to date her too. We've been together for almost a year.

JOSH. Rachel…

RACHEL. How can you do this to me? Everyone at school thinks I'm a joke.

JOSH. No they don't. *(beat)* Rachel, that thing you wrote just now…it sounded a lot like the trash that someone is writing about Cathy on Facebook. Is it you?

RACHEL. No!

JOSH. I think it is. Rachel, I think we should take a break.

RACHEL. No! *(begins to cry)* No, Josh, I'll stop. I'm sorry, I didn't mean it.

JOSH. So it *was* you, writing all those terrible things.

RACHEL. Yes! But it's the truth. Everyone says she's a ho, that she has sex with you so you'll date her… Why can't you see her for what she is?

JOSH. That's not true, Rach. She's a nice girl and we have fun.

RACHEL. Is that why you don't like me anymore, Josh? Because I let you…..you know.

JOSH. I still like you, Rach. It's just that I don't like you *that way* anymore.

RACHEL. Please, Josh, don't break up with me… please. You can date whoever you want… just… please…

JOSH. Rachel, we need to break up. I'm sorry.

RACHEL. *(enraged)* Okay! Fine! But you'll be sorry…you'll both be sorry.

> *(**RACHEL** disconnects and throws **HER** phone down.)*

RACHEL. *(crying)* You'll see. I'll show you both. If I can't have him nobody will. You just wait, ho, I'll get you for this!

Scene Five

At Rise: Several days later. Somewhere on the street.

*(**CATHY** and **JOSH** enter, arms around each other as **THEY** walk and talk. **THEY** are wrapped up in each other.)*

JOSH. That was a sick movie, wasn't it? Did you like it?
RACHEL. I loved it too. Except for all that blood.
JOSH. *(laughing)* You are such a *girl*.

*(**THEY** laugh together. **RACHEL** and her friend, **BETHANY**, enter from the other side.)*

RACHEL. *(sneering)* Look who's coming.
BETHANY. The love birds.
RACHEL. The *ho* who stole my boyfriend.
BETHANY. Yeah, right.
RACHEL. It's now or never.
BETHANY. What do you mean?
RACHEL. Just watch. Cathy-the-cow is going to get what she deserves.

*(**RACHEL** begins to dig around in her purse. **JOSH** and **CATHY** have come within a few feet of the other **GIRLS**.)*

CATHY. Hello, Rachel, Bethany.
JOSH. *(to the girls)* How's it going?
BETHANY. *(uneasy)* Uh…Hi Josh. Hello, Cath.
RACHEL. B-yatch!! Slut! I'm gonna kill you!

*(**RACHEL** snatches **HER** hand out of **HER** purse. **SHE** is holding a deadly looking knife. **RACHEL** lunges at **CATHY**. There is pandemonium. **CATHY** screams and lurches back away from **RACHEL** and the knife.)*

JOSH. *(stepping forward)* What the….? *Rachel!*
RACHEL. *(to Josh)* I'm gonna kill her! She can't have you!
BETHANY. *(screaming) Rachel! What are you doing?*
RACHEL. *(slashes the knife down)* I hate you! You took Josh from me! He's mine!

(JOSH has stepped in front of CATHY. HE grabs RACHEL's wrist and holds on.)

JOSH. Stop it, Rach! Give me the knife.
RACHEL. No! that b-yatch can't have you. You're mine!

(THEY struggle. JOSH wraps HIS other arm around RACHEL's waist while still holding HER knife hand. RACHEL suddenly wilts and all the rage goes out of HER. JOSH takes the knife and throws it away.)

RACHEL. *(crying)* I love you, Josh. And she took you away from me. I hate her!
JOSH. That's enough. Cathy didn't do anything. If you have to be mad at someone, you should be mad at me.
RACHEL. No, no, I *love* you.
BETHANY. I am so outta here. Rach, you need to get some help. *(to Josh and Cathy)* Sorry, guys.

(BETHANY exits. CATHY walks closer to RACHEL.)

CATHY. Rachel, I am so sorry. I didn't want you to be hurt.
RACHEL. *(hissing)* Get away from me, you slut. Ho!
JOSH. *(shaking her)* Stop it, Rach! It's over, do you hear me?
CATHY. Should we call someone, Josh? Her parents?
RACHEL. No! No!
JOSH. We can't leave you like this, Rach.
RACHEL. You don't care….nobody cares about me.
JOSH. That's not true. *(beat)* Cathy, I think we should drive her home.
CATHY. I agree.
JOSH. You drive, will you? I'll sit in the back with her. I'm worried that she'll….
CATHY. I know…you don't have to say it.
JOSH. Thanks. *(to Rachel, putting his arm around her shoulders)* Come on, Rach, we'll take you home.
RACHEL. Will you, Josh? I'm so tired all of a sudden.

(THEY begin to exit.)

JOSH. We have to talk to your parents, Rach, honey.
RACHEL. *(notices Cathy is still there)* Does *she* have to come with us, Josh?
JOSH. Yes.
RACHEL. Oh, all right. But, you know, I don't like her very much.
JOSH. I know. But, everything is going to be better, Rach. Let's just get you home.
RACHEL. *(snuggles next to him)* You're so good to me, Josh. You're the best boyfriend ever.

JOSH. I know.

    *(***JOSH** *and* **CATHY** *exchange looks over* **RACHEL***'s head as* **THEY**   exit.)*

CURTAIN

Glossary

Since Ms. Sugarek's scripts enjoy international sales this glossary is meant as an urban/internet dictionary for outside the USA where, perhaps, English is not the first language.

PROB - problem
IM - text
BRB - be right back
HW - homework
LOL - laugh out loud
C U - see you
Ridiculous - Fabulous, wonderful, cool
BFF - best friends forever
OMG - oh, my God
Sick - Wonderful, cool, great
BTW - by the way

The Art of Murder

CAST OF CHARACTERS

Montgomery...an unknown artist in Greenwich Village.

Detective O'ROARKE...a homicide detective with the NYPD

Samantha *(Voice (Off.))*... the woman that Montgomery is obsessed with.

Voices (Off.):   Voices from the street.

PRODUCTION NOTES

This could be a wonderful collaboration between the drama department and the arts department. The art students could paint several portraits of the same woman. In different styles and degrees of completion.

The profanity can be deleted.

Scene One

At Rise: A loft studio in Greenwich Village. Late afternoon. While there are many paintings it is apparent that one portrait has been done again and again.

(MONTY is painting at his easel. HE is a little paint smeared. HE hears voices from the street.)

VOICE *(Off.)* Hey, beautiful! You're home early.

(Brush in one hand, palette in the other, MONTY crosses to the windows and peers into the street below. The lilting laughter of a young woman is heard.)

SAMANTHA. *(Voice Off.)* *(joking)* Hey, Murray. Your wife know you're trying to pick up women in the street?
VOICE *(Off.)* No…..and don't you tell on me. My old woman would give me what for….bothering a young lady like you.
SAMANTHA. *(Voice Off.)* Your secret is safe with me…for a price.
VOICE *(Off.)* *(teasing)* Oh yeah, what's that?
SAMANTHA. *(Voice Off.)* Some fresh bagels from your bakery.
VOICE *(Off.)* You got a deal…I'll bring them home with me tomorrow.
SAMANTHA. *(Voice Off.)* Thanks, Murray! I'll look forward to them. Bye, now.
VOICE *(Off.)* Bye, beautiful. See you later.

(MONTY's shoulders slump and HE sighs. HE crosses back to his easel.)

MONTY. *(to himself aloud)* Jeez…how can that old guy be so easy with her. Monty, you're pathetic. You can't even say 'hello' to her in the street. What the fuck's the matter with you?

(MONTY resumes to paint for a few beats. A door slams down on the street and a woman's voice is heard.)

VOICE *(Off.)* Hello, Samantha. Where're you off to in such a rush?

(MONTY rushes to the windows and looks down.)

SAMANTHA. *(Voice Off.)* Hi, Mrs. Jessup. Just got a call. They want me to audition. Do I look all right?
VOICE *(Off.)* You're a blonde now, dear. And so quick!
SAMANTHA. *(Voice Off.)*   It's a..um…a wig..for the audition.

VOICE *(Off.)* Well, brunette or blonde, You look lovely, as always.

SAMANTHA. *(Voice Off.)* Do you need anything from the market? I'm stopping by on my way home.

VOICE *(Off.)* A quart of milk, if you can, dear. And a half pound of locks if it's fresh.

SAMANTHA. *(Voice Off.)* You got it, Mrs. J.

VOICE *(Off.)* Wait just a moment, I'll get my pocket book.

SAMANTHA. *(Voice Off.)* No, it's okay. You can pay me when I get home. Gotta go…..see you later.

VOICE *(Off.)* You're such a good girl. Bye.

>   *(**MONTY** watches a beat and then rushes back to **HIS** easel. **HE** carelessly discards the canvas on **HIS** easel and grabs a fresh one.)*

MONTY. *(to himself)* Spectacular! A blonde in a red dress. I must paint her rushing down the street, her skirt swirling around her knees.

>   *(**MONTY** dashes some red paint on the canvas; picking up a new brush, **HE** begins the blonde hair.)*

MONTY. *(to himself)* She's so damn pretty and so good to the old folks on the street. I have got to find a way to meet her without looking like a total doofus.

>   *(**HE** wanders back to the window and stars out longingly.)*

MONTY. Maybe, if I asked her, Mrs. Jessup would introduce us.

Scene Two

At Rise: The studio. Early morning.

(**MONTY** *sits at a small table.* **HE** *is rumpled and* **HIS** *hair is spiky from sleeping on it.* **HE** *holds a cup of coffee with both hands. A knock at the door.* **MONTY** *rises and crosses.*)

MONTY. *(Grumbling to himself)* Shit, who can that be?

(**MONTY** *unlocks a few locks and opens the door. A tall, handsome man, in a suit and tie is standing there.* **HE** *flashes* **HIS** *badge.*)

O'ROARKE. Montgomery Anderson?
MONTY. Yes.
O'ROARKE. I'm Detective O'Roarke. NYPD Homicide.
MONTY. Huh?
O'ROARKE. NYPD, Homicide. Can I come in?
MONTY. NYPD….like in police? I don't understand.
O'ROARKE. If I could just come in and explain and ask you a few questions?

(**MONTY** *backs up and opens the door wider in a gesture of inviting the detective in.* **O'ROARKE** *enters and* **MONTY** *closes the door.*)

MONTY. What's this about?
O'ROARKE. Do you know a Miss Samantha Sparks?
MONTY. *(looking guilty)* Well, yes and no. I've never met her….

(**O'ROARKE** *looks around the studio.*)

O'ROARKE. Really?
MONTY. *(following his gaze)* Yeah, I paint her a lot but I've never really officially met her….she's a neighbor…. *(he trails off, embarrassed)* ….why?
O'ROARKE. She's been murdered.
MONTY. *WHAT!?*
O'ROARKE. Last night…in her apartment…across the street.
MONTY. *(dumbfounded)* What?.....why??

*(Tears fill **MONTY**'s eyes. **HE** covers them with his hand but not before **O'ROARKE** sees them.)*

O'ROARKE. Can I get you something? Do you want to sit down?

*(**MONTY** stumbles to a chair and sits down.)*

MONTY. What happened?
O'ROARKE. We don't know yet. How well did you know her.
MONTY. Not at all.
O'ROARKE. It looks like you did….

*(**O'ROARKE** gestures to all of the paintings.)*

MONTY. I didn't.
O'ROARKE. It looks like she sat for you many times.
MONTY. No.

*(**MONTY** and **O'ROARKE** stare at one another. **MONTY** is too embarrassed to explain.)*

O'ROARKE. Look, kid. It's a bad idea to lie to the police. *(motioning to the many canvases)* You've obviously been painting her for months.
 MONTY. I know it sounds strange, but I've never even spoken to her.
O'ROARKE. And later you have a bridge you want to sell me?
MONTY. It's the truth.
O'ROARKE. Okay, let's say I believe that. How do you explain all these paintings?

*(**MONTY** is mortified. **HE** hangs **HIS** head.)*

MONTY. *(whispers)* I watch her from my windows.
O'ROARKE. What?
MONTY. *(raising his head)* I would watch her come and go from my window and then paint her from memory.
O'ROARKE. I see.
MONTY. I know I sound like some kind of perv. I wanted to meet her but the timing was always….just… off.
O'ROARKE. When did you last 'see' her?
MONTY. Yesterday…afternoon. She was rushing out to an audition.
O'ROARKE. Where? Do you know?
MONTY. No…I told you I have never spoken to her.
O'ROARKE. Then how….?
MONTY. *(more embarrassed)* I listen to her when she talks to the neighbors….down on the street.
O'ROARKE. I see.

MONTY. *(runs his hands through his hair) Fuck*! I must sound like a total nut case to you.

O'ROARKE. *(trying to sound sincere)* Not at all.

MONTY. …but I didn't hurt her. I never would.

O'ROARKE. Do you remember who she was talking to yesterday?

MONTY. Mrs. Jessup. She lives in Samantha's building. First floor.

O'ROARKE. You sound awfully sure.

MONTY. I've lived here three years, I know all the neighbors.

O'ROARKE. Except Ms. Sparks.

MONTY. Yes.

O'ROARKE. Okay. Let's leave that for now. *(Beat)* Do you watch out your windows a lot?

MONTY. *(hangs his head)* Yes.

O'ROARKE. Can you remember anything, say in the last week or two, that bothered you? Struck you as strange?

MONTY. Nooo….I don't think so. There were some taggers last week, late, but I yelled at them and they ran away. Just a couple of punks.

O'ROARKE. What about Ms. Sparks? See anything that stood out?

MONTY. *(Lying)* No. *(Beat)* Look, I've got to get back to my work. Are you done?

O'ROARKE. You're not telling me everything, Montgomery.

MONTY. I don't know anything!

O'ROARKE. Okay. If you want to play it that way, then we'll take it down town. Get your coat.

MONTY. *What?*

O'ROARKE. We need to go to the precinct so we can talk further. By the way, you never said where you were last night, between midnight and three AM.

MONTY. I was right here. Painting.

O'ROARKE. Did anyone see you here? 'Painting'? Roommate?

MONTY. No. I live alone.

O'ROARKE. Okay. Well, if you'll get your coat we'll go. Shouldn't take more than a couple of hours.

MONTY. Are you serious?

O'ROARKE. Serious as cancer…you'll need to give your formal statement. Maybe a polygraph…you know… to eliminate you as a suspect.

MONTY. But I told you, I don't know anything.

O'ROARKE. Yeah, you told me. So let's take down your statement that you don't know anything.

(**MONTY** *grabs* **HIS** *coat and* **THEY** *exit. The studio is empty as we hear* **VOICES** *from the street.)*

VOICE *(Off.)* Monty! What's going on, dear? Where are you going?

MONTY. Mrs. Jessup, don't worry, it's all a big mistake.

VOICE *(Off.)* But aren't you part of the police? What are you doin' with a fine boy like our Monty?

MONTY. Mrs. J. Can you called your brother-in-law? He's a lawyer, isn't he?

VOICE *(Off.)* Yes dear. But why would you need Leon? *(Beat)* Hey, Mr. Copper, you let him go now you hear? He's got nothin' to do with that nasty business that happened upstairs.

O'ROARKE. Stand aside, please Ma'am.

VOICE *(Off.)* I will not!   What do you think you're gonna do with our Monty, here?

O'ROARKE. Ma'am, you're interfering with police business.   And you could get into trouble.

MONTY. Please, Mrs. J., just call your brother-in-law. We're going to the…..*(he looks at O'ROARKE for the information)*

O'ROARKE. We'll be at the sixth precinct.

MONTY. Will you call him, Mrs. J.

VOICE *(Off.)* Of course I will, dear boy. Not to worry.

Scene Three

At Rise: An hour later. The police precinct.

(Downstage, left. **MONTY** *head in* **HIS** *hands, sits at a small table in an interrogation room.* **O'ROARKE** *enters and sits across from* **MONTY**.*)*

O'ROARKE. Okay, Montgomery.
MONTY. I go by Monty.
O'ROARKE. 'Monty'. You've been read your rights?
MONTY. Yes….but…
O'ROARKE. And you understand them?
MONTY. Yes, but…
O'ROARKE. And you agree to talk to me until your attorney gets here?
MONTY. Yes. I didn't *do* anything.
O'ROARKE. Let's just go through it again. Where were you between midnight and three AM?
MONTY. At home.
O'ROARKE. Alone?
MONTY. Yes. I told you, I was painting until late.
O'ROARKE. And no one saw you?
MONTY. No…oh wait…
O'ROARKE. Yes?
MONTY. Mr. Murray saw me around nine just before he went in for the night.
O'ROARKE. Mr. Murray?
MONTY. A neighbor. He lives in Samantha's building.
O'ROARKE. How?
MONTY. Huh?
O'ROARKE. How did you see each other? Were you leaving your apartment?
MONTY. No…no. From the window. Mr. Murray usually looks up and waves to me, or yells 'goodnight' …that's how.
O'ROARKE. And did Mr. Murray know the deceased?
MONTY. Who? Oh, Samantha. Please don't call her that.
O'ROARKE. Did Mr. Murray know *Samantha*?
MONTY. Yes, all the old folks in the block knew her. She looked out for them.
O'ROARKE. In what way?
MONTY. Oh, you know…picked up things at the market for them, made sure Mrs. J. took her medication. She always forgets.
O'ROARKE. Nice girl, huh?
MONTY. *(hangs his head in sadness)* She is…*was*…lovely.

O'ROARKE. *(switching subjects abruptly)* Tell me, were you upset when she changed her hair color?

MONTY. Why would I be?

O'ROARKE. You being an artist and all. Painting her so many times as a brunette.

MONTY. No, I didn't care. *(motions to the unfinished canvas across the room.)* Besides, it was only a wig.

O'ROARKE. *(raises his eyebrows)* Really? How would you know that?

MONTY. I heard her….tell Mrs. J.

O'ROARKE. From your….?

MONTY. ….window, yeah.

O'ROARKE. And you said you never left your place last night?

MONTY. I did. Leave, that is.

O'ROARKE. You did? You told me you didn't.

MONTY. I forgot. I ran down to the deli on the corner to get something to eat.

O'ROARKE. What time was that?

MONTY. Around seven?

O'ROARKE. Anybody see you? Mr. Murray for example?

MONTY. No, he was in his house eating dinner. He usually comes out after… for a smoke.

O'ROARKE. What time did you get back.

MONTY. Seven-twenty? Seven-thirty? I just grabbed some take out and came home. I didn't want to leave my paints too long…they dry out.

O'ROARKE. I see. How long did you paint last night.

MONTY. I think it must have been four…when I finally went to bed.

O'ROARKE. And you didn't see anything? Hear anything from across the street?

MONTY. No.

O'ROARKE. I have to tell you, Monty, I find that really strange….a guy who watches the comings and goings of the entire block, day after day from his window, and then sees nothing, hears nothing, on the night that a girl is murdered.

*(**MONTY** looks down at his hands and is silent.)*

O'ROARKE. Okay. Let's talk about what went on in the neighborhood in the last month. Can you remember anything that was out of the ordinary?

MONTY. No…I *told* you. It's a quiet street…nothing ever happens…the neighbors look out for each other.

O'ROARKE. You see quite a bit from your window, huh?

MONTY. Yes.

O'ROARKE. You see Samantha go out on dates?

MONTY. Yeah, sometimes.

O'ROARKE. How did that make you feel?

MONTY. Like shit…okay? I liked her and it made me feel like shit.

O'ROARKE. Did she have a regular boyfriend? Or did she play the field?

MONTY. What's that supposed to mean?

O'ROARKE. Did she have more than one guy coming around? She was beautiful, it wouldn't surprise me….

MONTY. *(angry)* No! She didn't 'play the field' as you put it and I don't appreciate you suggesting that she was…. cheap.

O'ROARKE. Okay, kid. Calm down. I have to ask.

MONTY. She hadn't been dating lately. She just broke up with her boyfriend about a month ago.

O'ROARKE. Really? How would you know that?

MONTY. Mrs. Jessup told me. Said 'now was my chance.'

O'ROARKE. Anything else?

MONTY. No. Yes….*(realization dawns on his face)* Oh…wait…I just remembered….he was there…

O'ROARKE. Who was where?

MONTY. The ex….on the street…about a week ago.

O'ROARKE. How come you didn't mention it before?

MONTY. I didn't…..remember.

O'ROARKE. So tell me what you saw.

MONTY. I was watching for Samantha because she was later than usual. I saw this guy sitting on a stoop a' couple buildings down. Didn't think much of it.

O'ROARKE. Okay. Anything else?

MONTY. So then Samantha came walking down the block. This guy, he stands up when she gets close. She stops, there on the sidewalk. She's frowning which is not like her.

O'ROARKE. Does she seem to know him?

MONTY. Yeah.

O'ROARKE. Can you hear what they're saying?

MONTY. No…they're down the block like I said. But…

O'ROARKE. Yes?

MONTY. She's not happy to see him.

O'ROARKE. How can you tell?

MONTY. She had her arms wrapped around herself. She looked tense like she was gonna run any second.

O'ROARKE. What's the guy doing?

MONTY. He's talking a mile a minute…his hands are flying around….*(he waves his hands around)* like to accent whatever he was saying, you know?

O'ROARKE. Excited like.

MONTY. Yeah, like that. And she is shaking her head, 'no'.

O'ROARKE. What else?

MONTY. *(Closes his eyes. Beat)* Then he grabs her arm. She pushes him away and I did hear her shout something but I don't know what it was she said.

O'ROARKE. And then?

MONTY. She walked away towards her building, kinda quick. Like just short of running.

O'ROARKE. And the guy?

MONTY. He just stood there…watching her. I kinda felt sorry for the dude.

O'ROARKE. Anything else?

MONTY. Yeah.

O'ROARKE. What?

MONTY. I'm pretty certain it was the ex-boyfriend.

O'ROARKE. Do you know his name?

MONTY. No, but Mrs. Jessup might.

*(**O'ROARKE** is silent for two beats. HE watches **MONTY**.)*

O'ROARKE. Anything else you can remember?
MONTY. No. Does that help….about the boyfriend?
O'ROARKE. It might. We'll look into it.

*(**O'ROARKE** stands.)*

O'ROARKE. Okay. I think that's all we need for now, Monty. We may need you again so don't leave the city unless you tell us first.
MONTY. *(standing)* I can go?
O'ROARKE. Yeah, you're free to go.
MONTY. *(relieved)* Okay.

*(**MONTY** exits. **O'ROARKE** stands, staring off into space.)*

Scene Four

At Rise: Later that day. The studio, empty. A heavy classical fugue is playing.

*(**VOICES** are heard on the street. **MONTY**'s voice sounds rushed.)*

FEMALE VOICE *(Off)*. Monty! Are you all right, dear?
MONTY. Yes, Mrs. J.
MALE VOICE *(Off)*. Wha'd the cops want with you, kid?
MONTY. Not much, Mr. Murray….just some questions.
FEMALE VOICE *(Off)*. Surely they didn't think *you* knew anything about poor Samantha?
MONTY. They have to question everybody, I guess.
MALE VOICE *(Off)*. Where you off to in such a hurry, Monty?
MONTY. Sorry, I can't stop to talk right now.
FEMALE VOICE *(Off)*. I'm sorry for your loss, Monty.
MONTY. Bye.
MALE VOICE *(Off)*. Wha'd mean, Mrs. J.? Monty didn't even *know* her.
FEMALE VOICE *(Off)*. That's how much you knew, Mr. Murray.
MALE VOICE *(Off)*. I know the kid was so shy he could even look her in the eye.
FEMALE VOICE *(Off)*. A bad business this is, that's all I'm saying.

*(**MONTY** enters, tearing off **HIS** coat. **HE** rushes to **HIS** latest canvas, sitting on the easel. Frantically **HE** opens tubes of paint and grabs a paint brush. Moaning and crying, **HE** stands looking at the painting of Samantha. **HE** loads a paint brush with bright, blood, red paint and slashes the painting with it. Over and over, **HE** stabs at the   canvas. With grief or rage?)*

CURTAIN

Song of the Yukon

CAST OF CHARACTERS

La Verne - The youngest sister of thirteen kids. She is barely sixteen and she yearns for adventure.

Robert Service - the ghost of Robert Service. La Verne and he are great friends.

Ivah - Her older sister. She is almost nineteen and engaged to be married.

Violet - Just eighteen, she is the sultry beauty of the family.

Author's note

Robert Service's poems are found in "The Best of Robert Service" Publisher: Dodd, Mead & Company, New York.

Based upon a true story, LaVerne did go to Alaska and did write her songs. This was developed into a novel also entitled '*Song of the Yukon*'

Scene One

At Rise: 1920. Late one night in the Guyer household. A bedroom shared by three sisters.

(IVAH and VIOLET, are asleep in the larger of two beds. LA VERNE lies on her bed, on the top of the blankets, while MR. SERVICE sits in a rocker. LA VERNE is dressed in a floor length night gown. A military-type duffle bag lies, almost out of sight, at the end of the bed. A single oil lantern burns to light the room. LA VERNE, her chin in her hand, listens raptly to MR. SERVICE.)

MR. SERVICE. *(Reciting his poetry.)* '*A bunch of the boys were whooping it up in the Malamute saloon; The kid that handles the music-box was hitting a jag-time tune;*
Back of the bar, in a solo game, sat Dangerous Dan McGrew,
And watching his luck was his light-o'-love, the lady that's known as Lou.
When out of the night, which was fifty below, and into the din and the glare,
There stumbled a miner fresh from the creeks, dog-dirty, and loaded for bear.
He looked like a man with a foot in the grave and scarcely the strength of a louse,
Yet he tilted a poke of dust on the bar, and he called for drinks for the house.
There was none could place the stranger's face, though we search ourselves for a clue;
But we drank his health, and the last to drink was Dangerous Dan McGrew.'...
..now go to sleep, little one.
LA VERNE. No, no, Robert. I'm not the least bit sleepy. Skip to my favorite part of your poem...please?
MR. SERVICE. What part is that?
LA VERNE. 'Were you ever out in the Great Alone, when the moon was awful clear'.....finish it, please?
MR. SERVICE. '*...And the icy mountains hemmed you in with a silence you most could hear;*
With only the howl of a timber wolf, and you camped there in the cold,
A half-dead thing in the stark, dead world, clean mad for the muck called gold;
While high overhead, green, yellow, and red, the North Lights swept in bars?-
Then you've a hunch what the music meant...hunger and night and the stars.

(THEY are both silent feeling the profound silence of the Yukon.)

VI. *(Across the room.)* La Verne! Wake up! You're talking in your sleep again! Shut up and go to sleep.

(VI flounces onto her side and buries HERSELF in the covers.)

LA VERNE. *(Whispers to Mr. Service.)* What most inspired you, Robert, about Alaska? The harshness of the landscape? The doing without...the hardships?

MR. SERVICE. No, no. I think it was the complete lack of concern by Mother Nature. You could live or die; she had far more important things to attend to. The stillness and purity of being totally alone out on the tundra.

LA VERNE. You want to hear my most favorite?

MR. SERVICE. Will you go to sleep after?

LA VERNE. (Reciting.) 'Men of the High North, the wild sky is blazing, Islands of opal float on silver seas;

Swift splendors kindle, barbaric amazing; Pale ports of amber, golden argosies.

Ringed all around us the proud peaks are glowing; Fierce chiefs in council, their wigwams the sky; Far, far below us the big Yukon flowing,

Like threaded quicksilver, gleams to the eye.' *(Rises and goes to the window and gazes out.)* ....and then my next favorite part.....

'Can you remember your huskies all going, barking with joy and their brushes in air;

You in your parka, glad-eyed and glowing, Monarch, your subjects the wolf and the bear.

Monarch, your kingdom unravished and gleaming;

Mountains your throne, and a river your car; Crash of a bull moose to rouse you from dreaming; Forest your couch, and your candle a star.

You who this faint day the High North is luring unto her vastness, taintlessly sweet;

You who are steel-braced, straight-lipped, enduring, Dreadless in danger and dire in defeat; Honor the High North ever and ever, Whether she crown you, or whether she slay; Suffer her fury, cherish and love her-- He who would rule he must learn to obey.' *(turns back.)* That's what I want, Robert, to rule and obey.

MR. SERVICE. Someday, little one, some day.

> *(HE rises and disappears. LA VERNE lies down. A few beats later SHE jumps out of bed and strips off HER night gown. Under it SHE is fully clothed. SHE puts on a heavy coat and a hat. SHE picks up her boots and duffle bag. SHE crosses to the large bed and pokes her sister's shoulder.)*

LA VERNE. Ivah...Ivah! Wake up.

IVAH. Umm...go away...it can't be morning yet. It's still dark out. Are you crazy, La Verne? Go back to bed this instant!

LA VERNE. Please, Ivy, wake up for just a minute. This is really important. Really, *really* important.

IVAH. *(Sits up.)* What is it? This better be important or you are dead. What?!

VI. *(Mumbling half asleep.)* Shut up, Ivah! Or *you* are dead!

IVAH. Oh yeah? And whose gonna make me? Not you...

LA VERNE. Shh...will you two be quiet? You're going to have the whole house in here.

VI. *(Burrowing under the pillow.)* Gladly. Get back to bed you two.

*(IVAH sits up in the bed, **SHE** plumps the pillows behind **HER**.)*

IVAH. Okay, squirt, what's so earth shattering that it can't wait 'till the morning?

LA VERNE. I'm leaving....I couldn't go without telling someone...I didn't want Mama to worry...

IVAH. Leaving? What'd ya mean?

*(IVAH takes in the scene and sees **LA VERNE** is dressed and sees the duffle bag.)*

What the h-e-double toothpicks is going on? You've got a coat on...what's in the duffle? What do you mean, you're leaving?

LA VERNE. I'm leaving...for the Yukon...tonight.

IVAH. Yukon? You mean in Alaska!? Are you nuts? Go back to bed. That's it! You're sleep walking...or I am. *(LaVerne pinches her sister.)* Oow...what did you do that for?

LA VERNE. You are not sleep walking and neither am I. I just wanted to say goodbye.

IVAH. Vi! Wake up this instant! La Verne thinks she's running away. Wake up!

VI. *(rolls over, leans up on an elbow.)* What the devil is going on? La Verne, why do you have your coat on?

IVAH. She's leaving, you slug. Wake up, I need your help.

VI. La Verne, take your coat off this instant and go back to bed. You're not going anywhere. You're the baby, remember?

IVAH. Shut up, Vi, and listen.

VI. *(Too loudly.)* Who are you telling to shut up?

LA VERNE. Please...you're going to wake up Mama. Maybe I better just go...

IVAH. No, no!

(IVAH pokes VI with her elbow.)

VI. Ow...stop poking me!

IVAH. Vi, La Verne has a problem, that's obvious. Let's be good sisters and hear her out. What's going on squirt?

VI. Yeah, spill it so we can go to sleep. It can't be that bad, Vernie.

LA VERNE. I've been thinking about this for a long time. I've read gobs on Alaska and that's the place for me.

LA VERNE. You can chase your dreams there, be whoever you want to be...no one's going to tell you what to do and what not to do...

VI. Let's get practical for a moment. How are you going to get to Alaska? Do you have any idea how far away it is?

LA VERNE. Oh, yes, I've done the research. I'm going to hitch a ride up to Seattle. Then I am going to sign on a freighter, working my way to Alaska. *(Sighing.)* That's how Robert Service got there.

IVAH. Just one little problem, Vernie. Robert Service was a guy. Who's going to hire a girl to work on a ship?

LA VERNE. I'm not going as a girl, dummy. I'm going to cut my hair and wear Eddie's old clothes. That way I can sign on as a kitchen helper or steward...I think that's what they call them. By the time they find out I'm a girl, either they won't care or it will be too late to turn back.

VI. Of all the hair brained ideas, Vernie, this takes the prize. *(flops down in disgust.)* Go to bed.

IVAH. Hold on there, Vi. Let's hear Vernie out. *(To Laverne.)* What's wrong, squirt? Why are you leaving us?

VI. Not that I wouldn't love to be rid of a pesky little sister.

LA VERNE. Everybody's leaving... Lillas got married and is having a baby. *(To Ivah.)* You just got engaged and when you get married you'll be gone. And Vi's on her way to San Francisco to play basketball. Everybody's having an adventure except me. I don't want to be left here all alone.

IVAH. You'll still have Pa and Mama...and the boys when they come home for visits.

LA VERNE. That's different. I won't have any sisters here. *(Beat.)* I'll be the only girl. Besides, I feel like...well...

IVAH. What? You feel like what?

LA VERNE. Different from you. I want different things.

VI. Oh, everyone feels like that at your age. I thought I was adopted, for a whole year when I was fourteen. It was the worst year of my life.

IVAH. You're just growing up, Vernie.

LA VERNE. No it's more than that. Different...

IVAH. How?

LA VERNE. *(Looks at VI.)* I'm afraid you'll laugh at me.

IVAH. No, I promise we won't. Don't we promise, Vi?

LA VERNE. Vi will laugh. She always laughs at me.

IVAH. Vi promises not to laugh. *(Pokes VI again.)* Promise her, Vi!

VI. Okay. I promise not to laugh, Vernie. Now what is it?

LA VERNE. I want to go to Alaska and write songs.

LA VERNE. See? She's laughing. I knew she would!

VI. *(Sputters.)* No, no...I'm not...it was just a cough. *(coughs.)*

IVAH. Just ignore Vi. You know how she is. Everything is funny except when it comes to her life.

VI. That's not true...

LA VERNE. Shhh...!!

IVAH. Vernie, I know you love your music and writing and all. I love the songs that you've played for me. But, can't you write them here? Mama loves your music.

LA VERNE. No. To be a great writer, you have to suffer. When Mr. Service went to Alaska, he got very sick and had to come home. It took him years to get better. *(Enthusiastic.)* He got dysentery, lice, and he almost died from pneumonia.

VI. Holy Christopher!   You're going to Alaska to suffer?   Stay at home and I promise to make your life miserable every day.   Now!   Can we go back to sleep, please? *(Sighs.)*   Good grief.

LA VERNE. You're mean, you know that Vi?   I knew you wouldn't understand.   I'm sorry I ever woke you up and told you.

VI. So am I, believe me, so am I.

LA VERNE. *(Wailing.)*   I...vah!

IVAH. Never mind her.   We all know how selfish Vi can be.   Just ignore her. *(Beat.)*   Vernie, have you thought about Mama? She is going to be so worried and hurt.

LA VERNE. That's why I woke you up, Ivy.   I thought maybe you could talk to her after I'm gone.   Make her understand.   Tell her not to worry.

IVAH. Telling her not to worry is like telling the sun not to set.   She'll never understand.   You're her baby, Vernie.

LA VERNE. See?   That's just it...I'm the 'baby'.   I've been the 'baby' my whole life.   I don't get to do anything. *(Beat.)*   I'm going all the way to Nome.

LA VERNE.   Just like Robert, I want to see the Aurora Boreattics, the...

IVAH. Borealis...

LA VERNE. Huh?

IVAH. It's Aurora Borealis.

LA VERNE. Yeah, that.   The wolves and the glaciers and polar bears, and the streams filled with gold.   Did you know that Robert Service rode with the mail carriers on their dog sleds? He traveled over a hundred miles with them delivering the mail and writing his poetry...

VI. He's a man!   Men do stupid and dangerous stuff like that.

LA VERNE. I don't care.   I'm going to ride with the mail and write my songs.

VI. Good grief.   *(flops over and pulling the covers up over her head.)*   There's no talking to her.

IVAH.   Do something for me, Vernie?

LA VERNE. I'm leaving...you can't talk me out of...

IVAH. No...I'm not going to try and talk you out of anything.   I just want you to wait one day...okay?   Let me think about all of this.   I didn't know that what our sisters and I are doing was upsetting you so much.   We've all been so wrapped up in our own lives and plans we haven't given much thought to how you must be feeling.

LA VERNE. Oh, Ivy, please don't blame yourself.   This is something I have been dreaming about ever since I was a little kid...I want an adventure...a big one!

VI. Good grief.

LA VERNE. *(Outraged.)*   Okay for you, Vi.   Everything is just perfect for you!   You get to go to a big city, play your stupid ball game, show off in front of a bunch of men.   Probably fall in love like everyone else around here and get married....

VI. *(sits up.)*   Whoa!   I didn't mean anything by what I said. I just meant....

IVAH. Oh, shut up, will you, Vi?

VI. Oh, like you know everything.   Just because you're marrying a big shot lawyer doesn't make you the Queen of the World...

LA VERNE. Well, she sure knows more than you do Vi.

VI. Well, thanks very much.   See if I bring you anything when I come back from Frisco...

IVAH. Anyway, Vernie.   Will you promise?   Wait one more day, okay?   Just one day.

(LA VERNE has put her hands behind her back and upon this request from IVAH, SHE crosses HER fingers.)

LA VERNE. Well...Okay, Ivy, I promise.
IVAH. Good girl! Now let's all get back to bed. I'll see you in the morning, squirt.
VI. *(Already half asleep.)*   'Night.
LA VERNE. I have to go to the 'necessary'.   I'll be right back.

IVAH. Do you want me to go with you?
LA VERNE. No thank you. I'll be fine.
IVAH. Hurry back. Don't let the bears get you.

(LA VERNE exits out the bedroom door.)

IVAH. Vi...Vi! You awake?
VI. Um-huh.
IVAH. Can you believe it? Vernie thinking she can get to Alaska? Of all the crazy ideas.
VI. Um-huh.
IVAH. You are going to have to help me talk her out of it. *(Silence.)*Vi? Violet Marie!   Answer me.
VI. Um-huh?
IVAH. Are you going to help or not?
VI. Yess!   Now leave me alone and go to sleep.

(Several beats. The GIRLS have fallen asleep. MR. SERVICE enters and sits in the rocking chair. The bedroom door opens and LA VERNE enters. Carrying her shoes, SHE crosses to her bed and sits down, fully clothed.)

MR. SERVICE. So, what are you going to do? I strongly urge you to dream your dreams for a few more years before you actually go...
LA VERNE. No. It's time. I feel it. I can't wait. It's like what you said in 'Dauntless Quest'... 'Why join the reckless, roving crew of trail and tent?
Why grimly take the roads of rue, to doom hell-bent? Columbus, Cook and Cabot knew, and yet they went.'
... Can you understand?
MR. SERVICE. More than you know. You remind me of myself at your age.
(Beat.)
LA VERNE. *(Turning to the two forms in the bed.)* Ivah? Vi? I've been thinking about what you said.   I think you're right. I couldn't possibly get to Alaska by myself. Ivy? Are you awake? Vi?
(Beat.) Okay then.

(LA VERNE rises and picks up her shoes and duffle. SHE quietly crosses to the door then turns back.)

LA VERNE. Goodbye. I love you both. Kiss Mama for me.

(SHE exits. MR. SERVICE rises and starts to exit.)

MR. SERVICE. *(To the sleeping forms in the bed.)* She won't be alone. *(Sighs.)* I shall go with her. *(Beat.)*   Vernie, wait for me.

CURTAIN

YOU'RE NOT the BOSS of ME

CAST OF CHARACTERS

Molly - 14 years old. The daughter.

Mother - 37 years old. A single Mom.

Bethany -15 years old. The most popular girl in school.

Optional: Various girls and boys - 15-17

Scene One

At Rise: A living room.

(MOLLY's mother sits on the sofa. MOLLY is sitting on the floor across from her. MOTHER is reading a book while MOLLY thumbs through a teen magazine.)

MOLLY. Mom! Look at this outfit! It's ridiculous! Can I go shopping?
MOTHER. Remind me again. 'Ridiculous' means good, right?
MOLLY. *(Sighs.)* You are such a tool, Mom. 'Ridiculous' means awesome, fabulous, beyond!
MOTHER. And 'tool' is a bad thing, right?
MOLLY. Well, not a bad thing exactly, but definitely a geek...or in your generation, *(Laughs.)* 'square'....yes, absolutely! You are 'square'. *(Beat.)* Can I?
MOTHER. Go shopping? Not for that outfit!
MOLLY. Why-eee?
MOTHER. Too provocative. Maybe when you're eighteen, not fourteen.
MOLLY. But, Mom, *(Whining.)* all the girls are wearing this.
MOTHER. Well, apparently not all the girls.
(Silence. Several beats as they read.)
MOLLY. Mom! Guess what?
MOTHER. Hmm?
MOLLY. Mom! Listen!

(MOTHER marks HER page and puts HER book aside.)

MOTHER. I'm listening, Molly.
MOLLY. Guess what!
MOTHER. *(An old game of theirs.)* How many guesses do I get?
MOLLY. *(Grins.)* One.
MOTHER. You bought a car?
MOLLY. *(Laughs.)* That is so lame. I don't even get my learner's permit for another two years.
 MOTHER. Oh, well. I guess I lose. What's up?
MOLLY. Bethany is having a slumber party next weekend...*(Dramatic pause.)... and* she invited me!
MOTHER. Bethany and that crowd aren't your friends....
MOLLY. I know! That's what's so awesome about it! Outta the blue she walks up to me after English.

MOLLY. I was at my locker, and she walks up with Courtney and Melissa and asks me if I want to come. I can, can't I, Mom?

MOTHER. We'll have to see...

MOLLY. *(Interrupts.)* Mom! You have to say yes. Those girls have never, even said 'hi' to me much less invited me anywhere. I have to go.

MOTHER. I'll call Bethany's mother.

MOLLY. Moommm! You can't! Bethany will think I'm a baby.

MOTHER. I'm certain the other girls' mothers will be calling too. And I am sure that Bethany's Mom calls the parents if Bethany sleeps over.

MOLLY. But, Mom...

MOTHER. That's the only chance you have of going.

MOLLY. Okkaaay.

MOTHER. Is Mary Ellen invited too?

MOLLY. No. She told me, when we were on the bus, that Bethany hasn't said a word to her. She's really jealous that I get to go.

MOTHER. How does that make you feel? She's your best friend.

MOLLY. Jeez...Mom…

MOTHER. Language.

MOLLY. Jeepers, Mom. I can't help it if Bethany didn't invite Mary Ellen. I love her bunches but she is a tool, ya'know.

MOTHER. And you're not?

MOLLY. *(Smug.)* I guess not. Maybe it's the new haircut you gave me for my birthday. *(MOTHER stares at MOLLY.)*

MOLLY. I don't know, okay?! I just know that one of the most ridiculous girls in school has invited me!

MOTHER. Before I call, I want you to think this through, Mols. Ask yourself why all the interest from Bethany and her group. Why now after snubbing you all through middle school. She must know you and Mary L' are best friends; why not invite her too?

MOLLY. Jeez...I mean..Jeepers! Mom! Do you have to make a federal case out of *everything*? This is so important and I have to go...I just have to!

MOTHER. All right. It's your decision. But, I want you to sleep on it. Tomorrow if you feel the same way, i'll call Bethany's mother.

*(MOLLY crosses over to **HER** mother and hugs **HER**.)*

MOLLY. You're the best!

Scene Two

At Rise: The living room.

(MOLLY sits on the floor. MOTHER is on the sofa with a cell phone on the table.)

MOTHER. So you've decided?
MOLLY. Absolutely! Bethany and Melissa and Courtney are being so nice to me. They see me in the halls and say 'hello' and they're laughing and so friendly.
MOTHER. Okay then.

(MOTHER dials her cell phone and waits for an answer.)

MOTHER. Hello...may I speak to Mrs. Pierson? Oh, hello, this is Mrs. Albrecht calling...Molly's mother? Yes, how are you? *(Listens.)* I'm fine. Bethany has been so kind as to invite Molly to her slumber party this Saturday and I wanted to check with you about supervision...*(Listens. Laughs.)*...Yes, they are at that age. The 'family room'? Oh, you are. Well, that's just fine then. *(Listens.)* Yes, I'd be happy to... What time should I pick Molly up on Sunday? That'll be fine. I'll drop her off around five o'clock Saturday then. Thank you. *(hangs up and turns to Molly.)* Both of Bethany's parents will be there. She has assured me that it's girls only and asked me to send some cupcakes. *(Beat.)* Well, that's it then. If you want to go, I guess you can.
MOLLY. *(Crosses and sits on the sofa with her mother.)* You are the most ridiculous Mom in the whole world.
MOTHER. I hope you know what you're doing. Just be careful.
MOLLY. What should I wear? Do you know where my sleeping bag is? Will you make chocolate cupcakes?

Scene Three

 At rise: The Pierson's family room. Loud punk rock blares. A disco-light flashes. Loud laughter and talking. There is smoke in the air.

*(**MOLLY** stands to the side watching as the other five girls and eight boys dance and drink. **BETHANY** approaches.)*

BETHANY. *(Laughing and tipsy.)* Isn't this ridiculous Molly? Why aren't you dancing? Want me to get you a drink?
MOLLY. No thanks. I have a Coke.
BETHANY. Whas' the matter? Don't be shy.   Hey! Look, everyone! Our Molly-Dolly is scared!
MOLLY. *(Bravado.)* I'm not scared.
BETHANY. Who's gonna dance with Molly?
Danny, come teach our little Molly some dirty dancing.
MOLLY. That's okay, Bethany. I don't want to dance.
BETHANY. Come on, don't be such a wall flower.
MOLLY. Really, I'm fine. You go ahead.
BETHANY. You are such a loser!
MOLLY. I'm sorry.
BETHANY. Did you actually think that I liked you? A total tool? Don't look now, Molly-dolly, but you're the party favor! Everybody likes a good joke. Hey! Everybody! Who wants a party favor?

*(**MOLLY** turns and runs from the room.)*

BETHANY. What a dweeb! Danny, my cup is empty.

Scene Four

At Rise: Later. Saturday night. The living room.

*(**MOTHER** sits on the sofa, feet up, reading a book. **SHE** closes the book, and stretches and yawns.)*

MOTHER. *(Mutters.)* Time for bed. *(Beat.)* Who'd a thought the house would be so empty and quiet with Mol's gone? *(Rising.)* Who knew?

*(Her cell phone rings. **MOLLY** enters far down stage on **HER** cell phone. **SHE** is crying.)*

MOTHER. Hello?...who is this?... Molly! Is that you? Molly! What's wrong?
MOLLY. Mom? *(Crying harder.)* Oh, Mom, it's awful.
MOTHER. Mols, what's happened? Are you all right? Molly! You've got to stop crying and tell me where you are...are you okay!?
MOLLY. Mommy...can you come and get me? Please?
MOTHER. Yes, yes, of course. Where are you? Are you safe?
MOLLY. I'm...I'm hiding under the back porch at Bethany's house. Mommy, it was all a joke, a trick...they're laughing at me.
MOTHER. It's okay, Baby. Don't move. I'm coming.
MOLLY. Mom! Don't talk to Bethany's parents...PLEASE! Just come and get me. Promise.
MOTHER. Of course. I'm on my way...don't move.

*(**MOTHER** rises and rushes out of the room, still talking.)*

MOTHER. It's going to be okay, Mols. Just stay where you are...I'll be there in ten minutes. Just keep talking to me...

*(**SHE** exits.)*

Scene Five

At Rise: The living room.

(MOLLY *sits on the sofa, wrapped in a blanket drinking something hot from a mug.* **MOTHER** *is sitting in a chair across from her.)*

MOTHER. Do you want to talk about it?

MOLLY. I guess.

MOTHER. We don't have to. Finish your hot chocolate and we'll go to bed. Things always look better in the morning.

MOLLY. Why do you always say that?

MOTHER. Because it's true. Because your wise, old mother has found that sleeping on something usually puts it in perspective.

MOLLY. Well, it's not true this time. My life is over. We'll have to move away. I can never go back to that school again.

MOTHER. That's why I think we should sleep on it. But, it's your decision; if you want to talk about it tonight...

MOLLY. I do want to...I don't know if I'll ever sleep again. It was so awful, Mom.

(MOTHER *rises and crosses to the sofa.* **SHE** *sits on the opposite end and puts* **MOLLY**'s *feet in* **HER** *lap.)*

MOTHER. Your feet are like ice.

MOLLY. It's okay.

MOTHER. Where were Bethany's parents, Mols?

MOLLY. They were there earlier. They came down and said 'hello' to all of us, before the boys got there.

MOTHER. Boys! But...

MOLLY. But I never saw them again.

MOTHER. Was there alcohol?

MOLLY. Yes, but I didn't want any. Then Bethany said I was a party favor...

MOTHER. Oh, honey...

MOLLY. *(continuing..)* I was a joke...they were drinking punch and acting silly. The boys were acting weird. Grabbing the girls and dirty dancing....Bethany and Danny were kissing and...

(MOLLY *shudders.)*

MOTHER. It's okay, Mols. Take your time. It's over now and you're safe.

MOLLY. Anyway, I was just standing by the wall, watching. And Bethany...*(Beat.)*... Bethany comes over to me and asks me if I'm having a good time. She tells the boys that someone needs to dance with 'Molly-Dolly'...that's what she called me. That and 'party favor'. I'm not sure what that means but it didn't sound good.

MOTHER. Oh, honey, I'm sorry...

MOLLY. That's when I ran away. I was so scared, Mom. Bethany and Courtney and the rest of them don't like me....I was just a joke to them. And then I ran...*(Wailing.)* ... like a baby.

MOTHER. The joke's on them, Mols. You acted with self-respect. You chose not to drink, you didn't do foolish things that you knew were wrong. I'm proud of you.

MOLLY. I'm not very good in the decision-making department. Mary Ellen tried to tell me...you tried to tell me. Going to that party was one, big, fat, BAD decision.

MOTHER. Now, hold on a minute. Maybe it was not the best idea, going to that party, but let's look at the great decisions you did make. You decided not to drink, not to get involved with those boys, not let Bethany and her friends pressure you into things that were wrong. You made another good decision by getting out of there and finding a safe place. And the best decision of all, you called me!

MOLLY. Yeah, I guess.

MOTHER. Honey, life is full of decision making. Sometimes we get it right, sometimes not so much...

MOLLY. Have you made some bad ones?

MOTHER. *(Laughs derisively.)* Oh, yeah, I've made my share. But the trick is to make more good decisions than bad. And learn from the bad ones that we make.

MOLLY. You're my BFF you know that, Mom?

MOTHER. Thanks!...I think.

CURTAIN

LOVE NEVER LEAVES BRUISES

CAST of CHARACTERS

Megan - 15, the girl friend

Tommy - 17, the boy friend

Pam - Megan's mother

Scene One

At Rise: A neutral place at school. A brick wall, under the stadium stands, or outside the locker room.

*(**TOMMY** has **MEGAN** by the arm. **HE** suddenly pushes **HER** hard up against a wall.)*

TOMMY. You were flirting with him!
MEGAN. No, Tommy, I wasn't. I promise.
TOMMY. I saw you. You're such a tramp.
MEGAN. Tommy, he's my lab partner. I was just kidding with him about our experiment exploding in class today.........
TOMMY. Bull crap. I saw you batting your eyes at him.

*(**TOMMY** grabs her by the shoulders and slams **HER** against the wall again.)*

Did he ask you out, huh? Did you say 'yes'?
MEGAN. Cut it out. You're hurting me.
TOMMY. *(Raising a clinched fist.)* I'll hurt you a lot worse if you flirt with another guy. You belong to me.
MEGAN. I know, I know. But, I wasn't flirting.
TOMMY. Stop saying you weren't.... I saw you with my own eyes.

*(**TOMMY** puts **HIS** hand around **MEGAN**'s throat.)*

You're a bitch...I ought'a....
VOICE (OFF.) Hey! You kids. Break it up! You're not supposed to be here. Where are your passes?

*(**MEGAN** breaks free and runs off. **TOMMY** runs the other way.)*

Scene Two

At Rise. Megan's living room.

*(**PAM,** Megan's mother sits on the sofa. A door slams and **MEGAN** enters. **SHE** throws **HER** backpack down and flops into a chair.)*

MEGAN. God! School is so lame.

PAM. Language! *(Beat.)* So, why is school lame today?

MEGAN. Lunch was gross, our lab experiment exploded and we have a re-do, and Tommy's acting all weird.

PAM. *(blasé to the complaints she uses the same cadence of speech.)* You took your lunch. You have to get a decent grade in chemistry. And....*(Picking up on the last complaint.)* ..... Weird, how?

MEGAN. I don't know. He gets all jealous and everything.

PAM. You're crazy about him. Why would he be jealous?

MEGAN. Charlie and I were laughing in the hall after chemistry. About our lab assignment shooting green slime on the ceiling.....

PAM. 'Onto' the ceiling....

MEGAN. Whatever. Green slime 'onto' the ceiling and Tommy came up and got all mad, gave Charlie the evil eye and stormed off. *(Beat.)* I wasn't doing anything!

PAM. Hormones. Tommy will get over it.

MEGAN. I'm not speaking to him until he says he's sorry. *(Beat.)* Have we got any food? I've got tons of homework.

PAM. I believe we keep that in the kitchen.

*(**THEY** laugh together. **MEGAN** exits.)*

Scene Three

At Rise: The next afternoon. The living room.

(PAM paces while SHE waits for MEGAN to return from school. A door slams off. MEGAN enters, drops HER backpack on the floor.)

MEGAN. I'm starved. Anything to eat in the house? *(Beat.)* What? What's wrong?
PAM. *(sits down on the sofa.)* Sit. We need to talk.
MEGAN. *(Sighs.)* Whad' I do now?
PAM. I don't know that you did anything. *(Beat.)* I got a call from the school this morning.
MEGAN. Jeez! I'm going to do the lab work over, okay?!
PAM. It isn't about your lab work. Mrs. Henderson called regarding what she called, 'a disturbing event'. She told me that school security found you and Tommy outside the gym, during classes, alone. No passes. Security told her that when he called out to you kids, you ran off like, let's see what were her exact words? Oh, yes, 'you ran off like a scalded cat.' Security told Mrs. Henderson that it appeared that you and Tommy were arguing.

(MEGAN is silent.)

PAM. Well? Is it true? Do you have anything to say?
(Silence.) Okay. You want to play it that way? You're grounded until you tell me what happened.
MEGAN. Moomm! Nothing happened. I already told you Tommy was jealous about the Charlie thing and we were talking about it between classes. Nothing happened! I ran 'cause I was late for class.

(MEGAN rises and starts to leave. PAM rises and quickly crosses to HER. PAM takes her by the shoulders. MEGAN flinches.)

PAM. Meggie, I just want you....What's wrong? Are you hurt?
MEGAN. *(SHE pulls away.)* No! No!
PAM. But you flinched. Let me see your arm.
MEGAN. Nothing's wrong with my arm.
PAM. Then you don't have any reason not to show it to me.

> *(**MEGAN** sighs and rolls up her sleeve. There are dark bruises on her upper arm.)*

PAM. What in the world! What happened?
MEGAN. I ran into a door, running for my English class, all right? Shish, leave me alone, why don'cha. *(She runs out.)*
 PAM. Megan! You come back here.

Scene Four

At Rise. At school. Lunch break.

*(**TOMMY** is sitting with **HIS** arm loosely around **MEGAN**'s shoulders.)*

MEGAN. I love you, you know that, right?
TOMMY. Sure.
MEGAN. So, we're cool, right?
TOMMY. Sure, Babe.
MEGAN. You got football practice after school?
TOMMY. Why do you want to know? So you can sneak off and meet that guy?
MEGAN. *(Sighs.)* No....I was just asking, okay?
TOMMY. Yeah, I guess. Did you get a new lab partner like I told you?
MEGAN. Tommy, I asked, I really did. Ms. Allen said lab partners are assigned for the semester.....no switching.
VOICE (OFF.) Hey! Megan. See ya in chemistry!

*(**MEGAN** gives her friend a half-hearted wave.)*

TOMMY. What're ya waving to that geek for? *(Beat.)* You like him! I can tell.
MEGAN. Tommy, why do you have to be so weird? Huh? I don't like Charlie that way. I love you.
TOMMY. What'd you call me? Weird? Did my ears hear you right? Weird? You're dating a football star, you stupid little tramp.
MEGAN. I'm sorry, I didn't mean anything by it. But, why do you have to be all jealous and mad and everything? Sometimes you act all crazy...

*(**TOMMY** punches **HER** in the face. **MEGAN** doubles over and begins to cry.)*

TOMMY. YOU make me crazy.... why ya gotta make me do things....why ya gotta make me so mad?
*(**MEGAN** jumps up and runs off.)*

TOMMY. Come back here. Meg! I love you. I'm sorry.

Scene Five

At Rise. That afternoon. The living room.

(MEGAN sits on the sofa. HER homework is spread on the coffee table. SHE wears a baseball cap with the bill low over her eyes. A door closes off. PAM enters wearing work clothes.)

PAM. Hey, Baby girl? How was school?
MEGAN. *(Her head down.)* Fine.
PAM. Fine? No complaints? *(Laughs.)* Are you sick or something?

(MEGAN slams HER book shut and piling all her homework into HER arms, SHE rises and starts to leave. As SHE passes PAM, head down, PAM lifts the cap off MEGAN's head.)

PAM. No hats on in the house, remember?

(MEGAN makes a grab for the cap and misses.)

PAM. Hey! What's with all the makeup? Is it that time of the month for zits?

(PAM takes a closer look. SHE gently takes MEGAN's chin in her hand and moves MEGAN's face up into the light.)

PAM. Meggie, what's wrong with your eye? Is that a *bruise*?

(PAM starts to rub off the makeup.)

MEGAN. Ooww! That hurts!
PAM. I'm sorry. *(Beat. Sternly.)* Go in the kitchen and wash your face, Megan. I'll be waiting here.

(PAM wearily sits on the sofa. A few moments later MEGAN enters. SHE has the beginnings of a black eye. SHE has the cap back on.)

PAM. Sit here with me, honey.

(MEGAN sits. PAM gently takes the cap off and looks at MEGAN's eye carefully.)

PAM. My God! What happened?

MEGAN. Nothing.

PAM. Meggie, I'm not mad at you. You can tell me. What happened?

MEGAN. Nothing! It happened at soccer practice, okay?

PAM. I know what a fist to the eye looks like, Meggie. I can call the school and speak with your coach, you know.

MEGAN. No! Don't do that!

PAM. Bruises on your arm. Now this? *(Beat.)* Did Tommy do this to you?

MEGAN. *(Scared, she begins to cry.)* NO!

PAM. Baby, you can tell me. Haven't we always told each other everything? *(Beat.)* Tommy did this.

MEGAN. He didn't mean to, Mom, honest.

PAM. Oh my Gosh! Tommy hit you?

MEGAN. He loves me, Mom. It's just that he gets jealous. He didn't mean to do it. He's always so sorry after. I say the wrong thing and then he....

PAM. Meggie, honey, I don't care what you might have said. There's no reason on earth a guy has the right to hurt you? Don't you know that? How long has this been going on?

MEGAN. Just a month or two.

PAM. *(Shocked.)* 'Just a month or two'.....

MEGAN. Tommy used to get mad and would call me names but he never hit me...well, this one time he did shove me. But, he's so sorry after and he loves me, Mom. Then Ms. Allen assigned me and Charlie as lab partners and Tommy got all weird about it.

PAM. So, Mrs. Henderson's call the other day? You and Tommy....?

MEGAN. We were just arguing and Tommy grabbed me by the throat....

PAM. What!?

MEGAN. So I wouldn't leave, Mom. And then security caught

> *(**PAM** realizes that **MEGAN** has been wearing turtle necks.)*

 PAM. Let me see.

MOLLY. It's nothing, Mom.

PAM. Let me see, Megan.

> *(**MEGAN** pulls down her collar. **PAM** can see the imprint bruise of a man's hand. **SHE** gasps.)*

MEGAN. Please, Mom. I love him. He loves me. Other girls' boyfriends get rough with them. It's no big deal.

 PAM. No big deal? Part of 'love' is respect, Megan. Love never hurts. Haven't I always told you that if you respect yourself, everyone else will too. If Tommy is putting his hands on you, he doesn't love or respect you.

MEGAN. But, I love him. Don't make me break up with him. Please.

PAM. Oh! You are so going to break up with him! Actually, I'm going to break up with him for you. That boy is never coming near you again.

MEGAN. Mom! You can't!

PAM. Meggie, this is the part where being the 'Mom' is no fun. I know you're probably not going to understand this but you are in serious danger. If you continue dating Tommy it will only get worse. He could hurt you very badly or even kill you.

MEGAN. *(Indignant.)* Tommy would never...

PAM. This is what we are going to do. First, we're going to go 'on line' and look it up. There's got to be a way to Google 'dating violence.' You don't have to take my word for it. Google it and see what other teens are saying. Next I'm calling your counselor at school and setting up a meeting with her, Tommy and Tommy's parents.

MEGAN. Mom! You wouldn't!

PAM. Oh, yes, I would and shall. You won't be there. If Tommy's parents agree to counseling for Tommy, I won't press charges.

MEGAN. You can't! I'll die of embarrassment. I'll never be able to show my face again.

PAM. Who's going to know? I'm certain Tommy won't tell anyone. You and I won't. So how are your friends going to find out?

MEGAN. They'll know. Can't we just forget about it? I promise I won't see Tommy again. Can we, Mom, please?

PAM. And what if a year from now you hear that Tommy has hurt or killed some other girl, Megan? How would you feel then about the fact that you didn't do anything to help Tommy?

MEGAN. You're impossible! I'm never going to tell you anything ever again!

*(**MEGAN** rises and runs from the room.)*

Scene Six

At Rise: Two weeks later. The living room.

*(**PAM** sits on the sofa reading the newspaper. A door slams off. **MEGAN** enters.)*

MEGAN. Hi Mom!
PAM. Hi. *(Beat.)* Are you speaking to me again?
MEGAN. *(Sheepish.)* Yeah. Can I have a snack before I start my homework?
PAM. There's warm cookies on the counter. Drink a glass of milk. No Coke.
MEGAN. Okay. Thanks.

*(**MEGAN** starts to exit. **SHE** turns back.)*

MEGAN. Mom?
PAM. Hmm?
MEGAN. Mom, I love you. You know that, right?
PAM. *(Lowers the paper and looks at her.)* What brought this on? I thought you hated me.
MEGAN. Tommy transferred to another school. I didn't realize until he was gone how stressed I was dating him. Now I know what you mean when you say, 'walking on egg shells'. And Charlie asked me to go to the game with him Friday night. Anyway... I just wanted to say thank you and let you know that I love you.

*(As **MEGAN** exits.)*

PAM. I love you too, kiddo.

CURTAIN

THE WALTZ

CAST OF CHARACTERS

Connie - An eighteen year old tomboy dressed in a gown.

John - A dashing young bachelor.

Scene One

At Rise: 1920's. A ballroom. A company dinner dance.

(CONNIE, barely eighteen and lovely in a coltish way, stands off to the side while the music plays. A new waltz is starting. A handsome young man approaches.)

JOHN. Excuse me, Miss Guyer?
CONNIE. Yes?
JOHN. I'm John Gibbons and.... Forgive me, I know we haven't been introduced but I'm a friend of Bill Murphy's and....well....I....with this crush tonight, I can't get him over here to introduce us. Anyway, I was wondering if you....
CONNIE. *(Nervous.)* Yes?
JOHN......would like to dance?
CONNIE. Well, since you're a friend of Bill's....I suppose it'll be all right....Yes! I would love to dance, Mr. Gibbons.

(The waltz music has already begun and JOHN takes CONNIE into HIS arms and THEY begin to waltz.)

JOHN. Bill says you work for his father.
CONNIE. Yes, I'm in the secretarial pool. May I ask? What is it that you do, Mr. Gibbons.
JOHN. I'm an attorney. I work at the firm that represents Bill's father's company.
CONNIE. Oh. How nice. *(Beat.)* It's a lovely party, don't you think?
JOHN. A little too stiff for my taste, if you'll forgive me for saying so, Miss Guyer.
CONNIE. Oh, no, there's nothing to forgive.   It's pretty snooty for my taste too. But the music's very nice. I love to waltz, don't you?
JOHN. Not until tonight. *(Beat.)* With you, Miss Guyer? I adore the waltz. *(Beat.)* Have you lived in Seattle your whole life?
CONNIE. Oh, no. I was raised in a little town outside of Olympia.
JOHN. Ah, our state capital. I have visited Olympia several times. My firm sometimes has a case that reaches the Supreme Court.   What's the name of your 'little town'?
CONNIE. You've never heard of it. Tumwater.
JOHN. *(HE grins.)* You're right, I never have. Is your family still there?
CONNIE. *(Laughs.)* Oh, yes.

JOHN. What's so funny about that?

CONNIE. When people ask about my 'family', they have no idea what they are getting in to.

JOHN. Intriguing.....give me details.

CONNIE. Well to start with....I have a lot of brothers and sisters.

JOHN. Really? I have two of each myself. Five kids. What a mob growing up.

CONNIE. Five? A mere pittance. Nothing remarkable in five....

JOHN. All right, Miss Guyer....out do me if you can.

CONNIE. Thirteen!

JOHN. *(Stops dancing and stares.)* What?!

CONNIE. Shall we continue? People are having to dance around us.

JOHN. Oh, yes, of course. Did I hear you correctly? You did say 'thirteen'?

CONNIE. Six sisters and seven brothers.

JOHN. *(In awe.)* Thirteen.

CONNIE. (Laughing.) Your mouth is open, Mr. Gibbons.

(JOHN snaps it shut.)

JOHN. Forgive me. I am stunned. *(Beat.)* Are all of the girls as lovely as you, Miss Guyer?

CONNIE. Oh, no, Mr. Gibbons, I am considered the ugly one....

JOHN. Then the other sisters must resemble Diana and Venus if they are more beautiful than you, Miss Guyer.

CONNIE. *(Blushing.)* Please, you're embarrassing me.

JOHN. I apologize. It's just that your eyes are so lovely. Your gown matches them perfectly. And may I tell you a secret?

CONNIE. Yes.

JOHN. I was terrified that I wouldn't get an introduction and some other man would sweep you into a waltz and you would be lost to me forever.

CONNIE. Mr. Gibbons, please, we've just met.

JOHN. I am sorry. Let me find a safer subject. *(Beat.)* Tell me, what does your father do?

CONNIE. *(Very proud of her father.)* He's a woodsman.

JOHN. Really? I'm not sure what that means.

CONNIE. He works in the forest. He's hired by people to cut trees and harvest the best wood. But he is very good at conservation and advises the owners of the trees about seeding and leaving stands of trees to propagate new growth....*(Beat.)*
Oh! I am sorry. I tend to go on and on about things....

*(The orchestra has begun a second waltz. **JOHN** and **CONNIE** continue to dance, oblivious to everything.)*

JOHN. Don't be. I find you thoroughly charming. You love your father very much. *(Beat.)*   And your mother?

CONNIE. She's the best. I admire her so much. She's strong, witty, beautiful and wise. *(Beat.)*
There I go again....I promise, I don't usually talk this much....you are just so easy to talk with, Mr. Gibbons.

JOHN. Would you even consider calling me John? I know that we've just met. It's probably too soon. I shouldn't have asked...

CONNIE. *(Interrupts him.)*   I would love to call you John...and you must call me Connie...John.

JOHN. You don't think me too bold? I wouldn't offend you for the world.

CONNIE. Not at all. Mama always tells me that I'm too bold.

JOHN. Well! Shall we be bold together?

CONNIE. *(Laughing up at him.)*   Yes, yes!

(JOHN twirls her round.)

CONNIE. Oh, stop, stop, I'm going to fall down....

JOHN. And I'm going to fall in love....

CONNIE. Oh, John, you mustn't. It's too soon.

JOHN. I know but I can't help it. You are so refreshingly honest, Connie. So genuine. The young ladies I meet are lovely people, I'm sure....but....well...they all seem to have this calculating gleam in their eye...and their Mamas... *(Laughing.)* ...make me want to run for the hills.

CONNIE. Oh dear. Why?

JOHN. I'm what's known as an 'eligible bachelor'. Very eligible, they tell me.

CONNIE. Oh, I see.

JOHN. No, you don't *see*. Please don't look like that. I don't want to be up on the marriage block, as my fraternity brothers say. I don't want a bunch of greedy mothers arranging a marriage between me and one of their daughters.

CONNIE. What does your mother say about that?

JOHN. Oh, she knows me too well to try to arrange anything. She's great! She's always let me make my own decisions. My Dad's a doctor and she was hoping that I would follow in his footsteps, so to speak. But, the first time I saw a court room there was no turning back for me.

CONNIE. When was that?

JOHN. When I was twelve. My Dad was a expert witness in a trial and he thought he'd take me along so I could see how cut-throat lawyers can be. Boy, did it back fire on Dad. *(Laughing.)* Talk about love at first sight. *(He gives her a meaningful look.)*   Say, twice in one life time. I've set a record.

(Beat.)   I want to see you again....soon. May I?

CONNIE. Yes...oh, yes.

 JOHN. When?

CONNIE. I don't know... next weekend?

JOHN. Oh, don't torture me...next weekend? That's too long.

CONNIE. John, you do know that we are being very improper, don't you?   You should meet my parents. But, they live four hours away, and oh, it's all so confusing.

JOHN. If you want me to meet your parents before we go out, I'll drive down to your little town of Tumwater. Don't you know that's the least I would do for you. I want to do so much more...

CONNIE. You may call me this coming week and we'll arrange....

*(Suddenly **CONNIE** stumbles....then stumbles again.)*

JOHN. Connie, are you all right?   What's wrong?

*(**CONNIE** has lost all beat with the music and stops dancing. **SHE** has felt something wrapped around her ankles. **SHE** looks down and sees that her drawers have fallen down around her ankles. **SHE** looks up at **JOHN** mortified.   **JOHN** is looking down and sees the same thing. Tears fill **CONNIE**'s eyes. **JOHN** speaks quietly so only **SHE** can hear.)*

JOHN. Connie, step out of them.
CONNIE.   Let me go, Mr. Gibbons. *(Struggling to be let go.)* I am so sorry....Please! Just let me go.
JOHN. Connie, do as I say. Step out of them.

*(Not knowing what else to do, **CONNIE** steps out of the offending underwear. In one quick motion **JOHN** bends down and scoops them up. Without a pause, **HE** puts the underpants in **HIS** jacket pocket and continues to waltz. **HE** dances until **THEY** reach the side of the dance floor.)*

JOHN. There. We made it with no one the wiser. I believe we will find the ladies room right over there. I'll wait right here until you have made the necessary repairs.
CONNIE. No, please, John, don't wait for me. I'm going home.

*(**SHE** puts out her hand and **JOHN** gives **HER** the drawers.)*

It was a pleasure to meet you.
JOHN. Connie, please, this doesn't change anything.
CONNIE. Oh, yes, it changes EVERYTHING!
JOHN. Changes what I see in your eyes? Changes what I feel? A little scrap of cloth?
CONNIE. Yes...'a little scrap of cloth'. *(Heartbroken.)* Goodbye....John.

*(**CONNIE** exits into the ladies room leaving **JOHN** standing there, dumfounded.)*

CURTAIN

Trans-G Kid

CAST of CHARACTERS

Kyler – Transgendered teen

Katharine – Kyler's mother

Gracie – Kyler's best friend

Bill —Kyler's Dad

In memory of Kyler Prescott
2000-2014

Scene One

At Rise: The library at Kyler's high school.

(KYLER *and his friend,* **GRACIE,** *sit at a table alone.)*

GRACIE. *(Dabbing at his cut lip)* Does it hurt?
KYLER. *(Flinching at her touch)* Naw. Not much anyway.
GRACIE. Sorry. I hurt you.
KYLER. It's okay. Has it stopped bleeding?
GRACIE. Yeah pretty much. Who hit you?
KYLER. Who said anybody hit me?
GRACIE. Come on, Kyl, you're talkin' to the expert on bullies.
KYLER. *(Shrugging)* Sam...Ken and that crew.
GRACIE. Creeps!
KYLER. It was stupid of me...I saw them coming and didn't turn around and leave. I was late for my next class. They jumped me before I knew what was happening.
GRACIE. They shouldn't be able to run the school like they do.

(Beat. **THEY** *contemplate the injustice of the school hierarchy.)*

KYLER. You still coming over to study at my house.
GRACIE. Of course. You still want to?
KYLER. Of course. *(Smiling, then wincing because of the split lip)* Just don't tell my Mom what really happened. I'm gonna say it happened in gym, during basketball. Caught an elbow or somethin'.
GRACIE. You don't play basketball.
KYLER. I did today.
GRACIE. You know I've got your back...I won't snitch. But you know you *gotta* tell your parents that this is going on, don't you Kyl?
KYLER. Yeah, I know. But my Dad will just tell me to fight back...man up. Or worse...I'm afraid they'll just transfer me to another school. That won't make a difference and I like Washington High.
GRACIE. You can't keep getting beat up. So what if you think you're a girl in a guy's body? Most of the time, I wish I was a horse.

(THEY laugh at **HER** *obsession with horses.)*

KYLER. *(Suddenly serious.)* I want to kill myself.
GRACIE. What? No you don't! Don't talk crazy.

KYLER. Gracie, I don't know how much longer I can pretend to be a guy. I don't think like a guy, don't feel like a guy, don't do normal guy stuff, and I love fashion and makeup. *(Glancing at her eye makeup)* Great smoky eye, by the way.

GRACIE. Thanks. *(She paused.)* Listen, you've got to get some help. You can't hide this from your parents forever and stay sane. What do you think your mother will say?

KYLER. I think she suspects. But she never says anything. She's great. Even, last year, when she came home early and caught me trying on her dress and shoes, she acted like it was cool. Asked me if I'd finished my homework.

> *(**THEY** chuckle.)*

GRACIE. I love your Mom. She's the best.

KYLER. I know, right?

Scene Two

At Rise: Kyler's family living room. A few days later.

(**KYLER** *sits on the floor at his mother's feet. His homework is on the coffee table in front of him.* **KATHARINE** *sits on the sofa leafing through a magazine.*)

KYLER. *(Keeping his head down.)* Mom.
KATHARINE. *(Flips a page.)* Uh-huh?
KYLER. You know how you're always telling me that I can tell you anything—anything at all?
KATHARINE. Yes. And that no matter what I will always love you. Don't forget that part.
KYLER. Yeah, I know.

(*Losing* **HIS** *nerve,* **KYLER** *is silent.* **KATHARINE** *sits up and reaching out, ruffles* **HIS** *hair.*)

KYLER. *(Smoothing his hair down.)* Cut it out, Mom!
KATHARINE. Sorry. I forget that you're all grown up, in high school and everything. Where did the time go?
KYLER. I dunno. Whad'ya mean?
KATHARINE. Nothing…it just seems like it was last week that you were toddling around the house with a droopy diaper. *(Beat.)* So? What's up, Peanut?
KYLER. *(Rolling his eyes)* Gross! *(Beat)* I've got something pretty serious to talk to you about. I don't know how to start.
KATHARINE. You finally going to come clean about how you got that busted lip?
KYLER. *(Blushes)* I told you… it happened in basketball.
KATHARINE. Since when do you play basketball? Come on…'fess up.
KYLER. How'd you know?
KATHARINE. I have super Mom powers. I know all. What happened?
KYLER. It's no big deal. There's this bunch of guys at school, jocks, and they roughed me up a little.
KATHARINE. 'Roughed you up?' I'd call a split lip more than a little horseplay.
KYLER. You gotten promise you're not gonna do anything about it. Promise, Mom! Besides, that's not what I want to talk about.
KATHARINE. Alright, for now I promise not to take action…not until I hear the whole story. *(Laughs nervously)* Please don't tell me you got a girl pregnant.
KYLER. Gross, Mom!
KATHARINE. *(Teasing, she smiles.)* Well! That's a relief.
KYLER. Besides I don't have a girlfriend.

KATHARINE. What about Gracie?

KYLER. Mo-o-m-m! She's just a friend.

KATHARINE. Okay. What's going on?

KYLER. I've got this huge problem and I don't know what to do. And I don't know if I can….if I want to…

KATHARINE. Kyler, baby, I'm your mother. You could murder someone and I would still love you. I wouldn't be wild about it, so don't kill anyone …I'm just sayin'….No matter what! I will love you and never, *never* judge you.

KYLER. Do you promise not to tell Dad?

KATHARINE. I can't do that. What I can promise is I won't tell Dad until you give me permission.

KYLER. *(He sighs and straightens his posture. Glances at her, then down.)* Okay, here goes. *(Beat)* I'm a *girl!*

> *(**KATHARINE**'s eyes fill with tears but do not spill over. **SHE** smiles sadly and takes **HER** son's hand.)*

KATHARINE. Kyls…look at me.

> *(**KYLER** raises **HIS** eyes and meets **HERS**.)*

Honey, I know.

KYLER. *(Pulling his hand away.)* What! Wha'd ya mean, 'you know'?

KATHARINE. Mother. Super powers. Knows all, remember? *(Smiling to lighten the mood.)* You're my son…I know pretty much everything about you.

KYLER. How long have you known?

KATHARINE. Since you were about four years old.

KYLER. *Come on.*

KATHARINE. Yep. We went shopping for pre-school clothes. You wouldn't put on a pair of jeans that I picked out. You ran over to the girls' section and picked out the cutest little pink dress. You were so happy, I bought it for you.

KYLER. You didn't.

KATHARINE. Sure did. *(Beat.)* So, when did you become aware?

KYLER. I think I was about seven. But, I didn't know what was going on. I really liked your outfits and I kept noticing women's clothes in store windows. I thought I was a freak. Turns out I am.

KATHARINE. Don't ever use that word again, Kyl! You are not a freak! Sometimes nature gets it wrong and you get put in the wrong body. *(Beat.)* I can't explain it better than that. But what I *do* know is you have a right to be happy and be yourself.

KYLER. Tell that to the rest of the world.

> *(**THEY** gaze at each other, knowing the enormity of **HIS** upcoming challenges.)*

KATHARINE. You'll be an adult in a few short years. What do you want to do? I support whatever you decide.

KYLER. I want to come out, Mom. I've been reading on-line. Turns out, there's a lot of us out there. But I'm scared, ya know? If I'm getting beat up now….think what's going to happen if I come out.

KATHARINE. We can change your school…that should make things…

 KYLER. No! I don't want a new school again. I want to be with my friends … Gracie…

KATHARINE. Okay. You can stay at Washington. Maybe if you do it gradually? …start wearing non-gender specific clothing…your hair will take some time to grow out…. *(She stutters to a stop; not certain what to suggest.)*

KYLER. When can I change my name?

KATHARINE*. (Shocked.)* You want a different name? … *(Checks herself.)* Of course you do.

KYLER. Do you think it will hurt Dad?

KATHARINE. That you don't want his father's name anymore?

KYLER. Yeah.

KATHARINE. It might pinch a little but your happiness is what counts. Have you picked out a name?

KYLER. Margaret…well, Maggie.

*(Beat. **SHE** stares at him.)*

KATHARINE. For my mother…your grandmother?

KYLER. Yeah. You think it'd be okay?

KATHARINE*.* I think it's a lovely name for you.

KYLER. Well, ya know, since I never got to meet her and I've always loved your stories about the crazy things she did as a kid, I like the sound of *Maggie.*

KATHARINE. She'd be thrilled, Kyls.

KYLER. Would you call me that…like now?

KATHARINE. Of course I will, *Maggie.*

KYLER. Again?

KATHARINE. *(Speaking with all the love in a mother's heart)* Maggie.

KYLER. *(Closing his eyes to savor the sound)* That sounds so—I don't know—so me. I am Maggie. Mags. *(Opens his eyes.)* But, never Marge.

*(**THEY** laugh.)*

KATHARINE. Your granny hated the name Marge too. *(Beat.)* You know, your grandmother would be so proud of your courage and wisdom.

KYLER. Really?

KATHARINE. Yep. *(Beat.)* There is one thing I would like you to do for me, Maggie.

KYLER. *(Suspicious)* What?

KATHARINE. Join a transgender teen therapy group.

KYLER. They have them?

KATHARINE. Yes. I think it would be good for you.

KYLER. A bunch of frea… *(His mother glares at him.)* Weirdos like me sitting around while a shrink tries to convince us we're all just going through a teen phase? No thanks, Mom.

KATHARINE. Not at all. I've done some research online also. The groups meet so that you, and others, can see you're not alone in this. There are others out there with the same challenges to face while going through the transition.

KYLER. Really?

KATHARINE. Really.

KYLER. That's pretty dope.

KATHARINE. So? Will you join one?

KYLER. I'll go *once* and check it out.

KATHARINE. Fair enough. *(Beat)* Well, when would you like to go shopping?

Scene Three

At Rise: Gracie's house.

(GRACIE *and* **KYLER** *sit at the dining room table, books and laptops in front of* **THEM.***)*

GRACIE. This was the most boring book I have *ever* read.
KYLER. I kind'a liked it…but it was long.
GRACIE. Ya think? Five hundred and some odd pages of blah, blah, blah.
KYLER. Three hundred, sixty five.
GRACIE. *(Sighing)* Whatever.
KYLER. I told my mom.
GRACIE. *(Eyes round)* Wow. What'd she say?
KYLER. She was so dope. Didn't even blink…well, she got a little teary eyed but she said she knew.
GRACIE. *She knew?*
KYLER. Yeah. Since I was in kindergarten.
GRACIE. Wow! What'd she say?
KYLER. *(Laughing)* Called me Maggie and wanted to know if I wanted to go shopping.
GRACIE. She's the coolest mom *ever!*
KYLER. I know, right?
GRACIE. Does your Dad know too?
KYLER. She's telling him tonight...while I'm over here. He's gonna have a cow!
GRACIE. Maybe…maybe not. With parents…you can never tell.
KYLER. What if he disowns me or something, Gracie?
GRACIE. He won't…your mom won't let him. Trust her to make it all right.
KYLER. How am I going to face him?
GRACIE. As Maggie. A strong young woman who knows herself and knows what's best for her.
KYLER. I don't know…Sometimes I think it would be easier if I just didn't exist…
GRACIE. You'll be okay. Always remember that I'm here and your Mom's supporting you. *(Laying her hand on his)* You gotta be who you really are.
KYLER. I guess.
GRACIE. When can I start calling you 'Mags'? I love your new name. I wish I had a cool name.
KYLER. What? Like Flicka?
GRACIE. *(Laughing)* I could do worse. Grace is so puritan.
KYLER. You can call me Mags starting tonight. But not at school. Wait until everyone knows.
GRACIE. Okay. Guess we better start working on this book report, *Mags.*
KYLER. *(Suddenly closes his laptop and gathers his books. He stands.)* I'm tired. I'm gonna head home. I'll see you tomorrow.

GRACIE. But…what about our book report?
KYLER. I'll do it at home. Bye.

*(**KYLER** rushes out.)*

Scene Four

At Rise: Kyler's family living room.

(**KATHARINE** *and* **BILL***, Kyler's father, sit in chairs talking.*)

BILL. Where's Kyler?
KATHARINE. Over at Gracie's doing a literature project.
BILL. *(Frowning.)* They spend a lot of time together.
KATHARINE. Thank God. She's good for him.
BILL. I guess. *(Beat.)* How was your day?
KATHARINE. It was good. How about you?
BILL. It was rough. I'm beat. But we did get the Johnson deal closed.
KATHARINE. I need to talk to you…about Kyler. I had a very serious talk with our son.
BILL. *(Perking up)* Is he in trouble?
KATHARINE. Bill, when has our son ever given us an ounce of trouble?
BILL. Never. But he is a teenager now. This is when it's supposed to start happening isn't it? Look at the Huntingtons …their daughter runs away every week. God, it's got to be a nightmare for Jim and Susie.
KATHARINE. Maybe if Jim paid her some attention she wouldn't be running away.
BILL. *(Sighing)* Please, let's not get into that again. Jim has to make a living and that living involves being on the road.
KATHARINE. I don't want to talk about the Huntingtons. I want to discuss our son.
BILL. Fire away. But, let me get some water first. You want some?
KATHARINE. No, I'm fine. There's a couple of bottles in the mini-fridge.
BILL. When's dinner?
KATHARINE. An hour.
BILL. Okay. Just a sec'.

(**HE** *crosses to the bar and, opening the fridge gets a bottle of water.* **HE** *crosses back to* **HIS** *chair and sits.*)

BILL. What's up with Kyler?

(*Unbeknownst to the parents,* **KYLER** *has walked in the back door of the kitchen.* **HE** *hears the low murmurs of* **HIS** *parents in the living room. Unable to resist,* **HE** *creeps down the hallway and listens outside the door.*)

KATHARINE. He's in crisis and he needs both of us to support and understand him.
BILL. *(Sitting up straight)* Kat, what the devil does *that* mean?

KATHARINE. Kyler isn't certain of his gender identity. Well, I take that back… he is *very* certain…he doesn't believe that he's a boy. He feels…has felt for a long time…that he is a girl. He wants to transition.

BILL. Transition what?

KATHARINE. *(Sighing)* Bill, he's transgender. I've just been waiting until he either discovered who he is or wanted to talk about it or…

BILL. Wait a minute. What are you talking about?…transition…he's not a boy?…what the H?! Is he having a breakdown? We can get him help. A psychiatrist, a counselor…

KATHARINE. He *is* going to need counseling but not to change his mind. Rather to help him through the transition. It's not going to be easy on him.

BILL. You're supporting this—this— craziness? *(Beat)*

(Out in the hallway, **KYLER** *hangs* **HIS** *head at* **HIS** *father's words.)*

KATHARINE. Bill! Shame on you! He's not crazy. I've been doing some research. About people whose gender identity and behavior doesn't conform to that typically associated with the sex to which they were assigned at birth. A person's internal sense of being male, female conflicts with their outward appearance. It has to be excruciating for Kyler.

BILL. Hog wash! That's a bunch of psycho -babble! He's been a boy for fifteen years! He's my son!

KATHARINE. Yes, he's put up a pretty good front.

BILL. What the sam-hill is that supposed to mean?

KATHARINE. That he's been fighting his true self for most of that time. He became aware that he was different at around age seven. He's tried to hide his feelings all this time and it's tearing him apart.

BILL. I don't buy it. It's just teenage hormones. Find a shrink that deals with this kind of thing.

KATHARINE. *(Sighing)* Bill. I never thought… *(Beat.)* …I started to say…I never thought you'd handle it like you are…but I realize now, you are reacting exactly like I thought you would.

BILL. I don't have a gay son!

KATHARINE. *(Raising her voice.)* He's *not* gay. He's transgender.

BILL. There's a difference?

KATHARINE. OMG, where have you been? Don't you watch the media? The T.V.? Just last week we watched the news together about that teenager who committed suicide because he couldn't be who he truly was. Is that what you want? To go to our son's funeral?

BILL. Calm down. I never said that. But that kid who killed himself was obviously messed up. Wasn't he being raised by a single mom?

KATHARINE. *(Shouting.)* What's that got to do with anything? The kid was transgender and his peers and the world around him put so much pressure on him that he killed himself.

BILL. I'm sorry…I didn't mean…

KATHARINE. This is your wake up call, Bill. We've got to get in front of this and give Kyler our complete support.

BILL. But…

KATHARINE. But what? Don't you see? That could be our dead son on the news.

*(***THEY*** sit and stare at each other. Beat.)*

BILL. I'm losing my son and I'm supposed to be *okay* with that?

KATHARINE. You're not. You're gaining a happy, well-adjusted daughter in his place. By the way, her name is Maggie.

BILL. He's giving up my father's name!?

KATHARINE. Yes. She chose my mother's name as her new name.

BILL. *(Pulling at his hair with both hands)* This is nuts! Don't I have any say about *anything* in this household?

KATHARINE. Yes. What is it that you want to say?

BILL. I don't agree with this craziness. I think we should put *Kyler* in therapy. He'll grow out of it. It's just a phase. When I was his age I wanted to be a clown in the circus.

KATHARINE. Bill. This is not a phase. This is as serious as a heart attack. Your son needs you.

BILL. I can't, Katharine. He's my son…he carries my father's name. How many times have we marveled at how like my father he is?

KATHARINE. That was what *you* always said. I always thought he reminded me more of my mother. Of course, I kept that little tidbit to myself because I feared that you would react *exactly* like you are.

BILL. You mustn't encourage him, Kat.
He's got some crazy notion that he's a girl? It's ludicrous!

KATHARINE. I hope you don't live to regret your stand on this, Bill. If anything happens to our son because of your attitude I will never forgive you.

BILL. Kat…

KATHARINE. I, for one, will support him in whatever he wants to do. I will call him—her—Maggie. I will take her shopping—I will fight the school if they don't support her—if she wants physical transitions I will pay for it…

BILL. *(Shouting.)* Over my dead body!

*(Rising from where **HE** had been sitting on the floor, **KYLER** crosses quietly to the door that leads to the garage. **HIS** shoulders are slouched in defeat. **HE** wipes **HIS** eyes as **HE** exits. As lights go down on the living room, **KYLER/MAGGIE** crosses and takes a length of rope down from a hook on the garage wall. **HE** stares down at it.)*

CURTAIN

TRANS-G PARENTS

CAST OF CHARACTERS

Parents in a support Group for transitioning children.

Amanda/George
 (Child: Joy)
 (Refused infant surgery to 'correct' ambiguity of genitalia)

Sally/Ben
(Child: Charlie)
(Lost their child to suicide)

Vince/Susie
(Child: Caitlin/Cade)
(Older; they have a son who has gone through entire transition)

Tom/Patty
(Child: Ruth/Roger)
(Their daughter insists she's a boy and, as they are
deeply religious, they are angry and confused)

Richard/Gloria
(Child: Richard Jr./Riley)
(Resisting their child's gender confusion)

Allie
(Child: Kyler/Maggie)
 (Single mother)

Scene One

At Rise: A group of folding chairs in a crescent shape face down stage. There is one empty chair.

(A group of **PARENTS** *sit together, chatting quietly.* **ALLIE***, a single mother, rushes on stage.* **SHE** *scuttles to the empty chair and sits.)*

ALLIE. I'm sorry I'm late. My car wouldn't start. Have I kept you waiting long?
SUSIE. Not to worry, dear. We were just getting settled.
VINCE. Shall we begin? Ben, Sally, when we broke last week you were sharing with the group. Your child took his own life due to bullying?
SALLY. Yes, five years ago. Charlie was very private. Only his best friend and we knew he was experiencing confusion when it came to his gender identity.
BEN. We thought he was doing fine, ya know?

(Choking up, **HE** *can't continue.* **SALLY** *pats his back.)*

SALLY. Rumors began at school and then started to hit social media. The bullying began from some of the older boys. We thought we were on top of it. We kept an open dialogue with him. As a family we went to counseling. But it wasn't enough. It was like he gave up, was too tired to continue. We found him hanging in his closet.
TOM. My sweet Christ, why is this happening to all of us?
PATTY. Tom! Please don't use the Lord's name in vain.
TOM. Sorry, honey, I didn't mean it like that. I really want to know. Why are all these kids, these days, walkin' around not knowing if they're boys or girls? Are they mentally ill or what?
VINCE. We're older than most of you and have been on this journey for many years with our Caitlin. So if I may, I'd like to try and answer you, Tom. *(He sighs at Tom's ignorance.)* Our children are not mentally ill. Far from it. They're smart kids and usually know from an early age that something is different. Call it gut intuition or whatever…they don't identify with their external genitalia. Our son, Cade, was picking out girl's clothing since he was five.
SUSIE. *(Smiling at the memories)* We'd go shopping for school clothes and he would run straight to the girl's department. *(Laughs)* When she was four, for a whole year, she wore a tutu around the house. I could barely get it off of her to wash it.
PATTY. Tom and I really don't understand. Ruthie's private parts and her soft hair and fine features all reassure us that she's a little girl. Now all of a sudden she wants jeans and shirts and wants us and her brothers and sisters to call her Robbie.
TOM. Over my dead body!

SUSIE. I know it's very scary for the whole family. Let me see if I can explain it this way; Transgender simply means a person's personal identity does not correspond with the gender they were assigned at birth. Regardless of whether they 'look' like a baby boy or girl as they grown up they don't identify with their external genitalia. I have a picture at home where Cade is all dressed up in his snow wear; I think he was about five. Over it all he'd pulled on a dress. *(She laughs.)* It was the funniest thing we'd ever seen.

> *(Most of the other* **PARENTS** *laugh at this image.)*

TOM. Excuse me and I don't mean to sound rude but I think some of you are too permissive as parents. They're *kids* for crying-out-loud. Parents tell their kids where to go, when to go, how to do it, and why. If God creates a little boy, he *stays* a little boy!
SUSIE. It's not rude to say what's on your mind, Tom. We're all here to help each other and, hopefully, ourselves. One day Caitlin had this conversation with me after years of wanting to dress in girl's clothing. At age eleven she told me, 'Mom, I'm a girl in my heart and my brain.' How do you argue with that when the alternative is much worse?
PATTY. But it's against everything the Bible teaches us!
TOM. *(He argues as if his wife had not spoken.)* And you allowed it?
SUSIE. Yes, Tom. We wanted our child to be happy.
PATTY. Disgraceful! The scriptures clearly state that it is a sin against our Lord!
SALLY. Would you rather see your child in their coffin?
BEN. *(Placing his arm around his wife)* Easy, Babe. She doesn't understand.
PATTY. Yes! Our Ruthie's going to hell anyway if she continues to insist that she's really a boy. I'd rather see her dead than disgracing herself in public, running around acting…dressing like a boy.
SALLY. *(Beginning to weep)* I hope your prayers don't come true, Patty.

> **(TOM** *rises and begins to pace.* **HE** *returns to his chair, grabbing it by its back, lifts it and slams it down to accentuate what* **HE** *is saying.)*

TOM. Blasphemy! A sin against God. I won't allow it! Ruthie will grow up to be a God-fearing woman, raised in the church. All this 'Roger' crap is just that….crap!

PATTY. Tom! Language!

> *(***SHE** *turns to the others.)*

Tom doesn't mean to offend. He's so upset. Our Ruth came to me and told me she was a boy trapped in a girl's body. She told me God had made a mistake. It broke my heart…God doesn't make mistakes.
TOM. Be quiet, Patty. I don't want to hear it. She's my daughter and she's just going through some kind of female hysteria.
RICHARD. I hear you. My only child thinks, all of a sudden, that he's a girl. I feel like I'm in a bad dream that I can't wake up from.

GLORIA. R.J. came to us just last week. It's all so new. We're so confused. He told us we should start calling him Riley and he has started wearing non-gender specific clothes.

TOM. What the hell does that mean?

(Some of the **PARENTS** *smile.* **VINCE** *chuckles.)*

GLORIA. I had to go on-line and look it up. I was shocked to find dozens of sites selling these clothes. I'm still reading.

RICHARD. I'm with you, Tom, my son is my son, end of discussion. Gloria dragged me here quoting some pretty disturbing statistics.

BEN. Suicide. I'm afraid those stats are real, Richard.

GLORIA. Oh my God.

GEORGE. Vince and Susie, here, have much more experience than all of us put together. Vince would you share with some of the new-comers?

VINCE. Our son, at the time, Cade, came to us when he was thirteen. That would be ten years ago. He was distraught. Susie thought he must have some terminal disease, he was so upset.

SUSIE. *(Laughs, remembering.)* Image my relief when it wasn't that my child was going to die but it was something we could work through.

VINCE. As a child he played with whatever toys were available. Dolls, trucks, whatever. He loved dress-up and tea parties with his younger sisters. But also owned a set of toy cars and played basketball. He was a well-adjusted kid and we thought nothing of his indulging his sisters and joining the tea parties. Anyway, when he came to us we immediately got into counseling as a family and hit the midnight oil researching what this meant for our son and to us as a family. We were advised to keep a very close eye on him during this early transitioning period. Warned that our son would be feeling scared and confused. The suicide rates were even higher ten years ago. Fast forward: *Caitlin* is now twenty-three, a senior at St. Mary's. She began hormone therapy when she was fourteen and began gender affirmation surgery when she was eighteen.

SUSIE. It's hard to think of her as a boy now. She's a lovely, successful young woman.

(Several beats of silence as the **GROUP** *takes in this story.)*

VINCE. How 'bout we take a coffee and restroom break. Five minutes okay?

(The **PARENTS** *rise and wander around. Getting star foam cups of coffee or bottles of water sitting on a back table.* **NO ONE** *leaves the stage for the restroom.* **THEY** *soon return to their chairs.)*

ALLIE. *(Tentatively raises her hand.)* I'd like to share if that's all right. As you know my son, Kyler came out to me last year. Maggie, my new daughter, has been through a lot. She doesn't dress all *girlie* or anything. *(She smiles at Gloria.)* But she has changed her wardrobe to non-specific gender. Her hair has grown down to her shoulders. I've allowed a little makeup…she's only fourteen. I went with her to the school and changed her name from Kyler to Margaret …Maggie.

SUSIE. How's it going?

ALLIE. She's bullied a lot. It's taking a toll on her and I'm frightened all the time. *(Glancing around at the group)* I don't think I could stay sane if I didn't have all of you.

AMANDA. All our situations are so different. That's why this group is so invaluable to all of us. The one common thread is that we have children transitioning to be their real selves. No matter how that manifests itself.

ALLIE. *(Hushed voice.)* We had the surgery when Kyler was born because that's what the doctors recommended. Thank God it worked out! But Maggie will need more to finish correcting her physical anatomy.

(**VINCE** *turns to George and Amanda.*)

VINCE. You and George opted against infant corrective surgery didn't you?

AMANDA. Yes. As some of you know when your baby is born and there is ambiguous genitalia, the doctors recommend doing corrective surgery within a few months of their birth. We refused.

SALLY. How old is your child now?

GEORGE. Joy is four now.

GLORIA. So she's? What?

GEORGE. Still ambiguous.

GLORIA. But…I don't understand. What will she say when she's old enough to notice? Ask questions.

AMANDA. Gloria, we wanted our child to be able to decide what gender she was. We are raising her as a little girl but we know the day will come that she will come to realize her true gender…boy or girl.

GEORGE. Right now she plays with dolls and trucks and hits a mean baseball.

RICHARD. But when that day comes, how do you justify leaving her…well, the way she is?

AMANDA. George and I decided we'd rather answer the question, *'Why didn't you do something when I was born?'* than *'Why did you do this to me?'* If we had opted for a clitoridectomy and she decided her gender identification was male we would have essentially castrated our own child. It was an easy decision to do nothing.

(**TOM** *bolts from his chair and rushes off stage.*)

TOM. I think I'm going to be sick.

(**PATTY** *jumps up and follows him.*)

PATTY. *(Running off stage.)* Tommy! Wait!

(The **GROUP** *watches the hasty retreat with varied reactions.*)

SUSIE. *(Shaking her head.)* It's really tough on all of us but for a family steeped in fundamental faith, it's beyond difficult.

SALLY. They must be very careful. Their faith won't save them or their child from the statistics.

(**VINCE** *rises and* **SUSIE** *follows.*)

VINCE. Good work everyone. The Yoga class will be here any minute so if you'll help stack the chairs against the back wall, we'll call it a night.

Scene Two

At Rise: The meetings for parents of transgender kids has continued. It is now several months later. Chairs are preset.)

(**PARENTS** *begin to trickle in for the group meeting. Three chairs remain empty.* **THEY** *sit down, quietly greeting each other.*)

VINCE. Shall we begin?

RICHARD. Are Tom and Patty coming? Do you know?

SUSIE. I was finally able to reach Patty by phone. She said that while she was open to coming back, Tom was adamant that it was a waste of time and I quote here, "God would take care of everything."

BEN. *(Bitterly.)* Good luck with that!

AMANDA. Has anyone spoken to Allie?

SALLY. I've tried to reach her several times but no luck. It's a terrible time.

RICHARD. I would like to say something, if I may.

(The other **PARENTS** *turn to* **RICHARD**.)

RICHARD. Gloria dragged me here *(Ironic smile)* over eight months ago. I was so angry. *My son!* He was no longer my son and wanted to be my daughter. I couldn't get my head around it. My pride was injured and my feelings were hurt. Why didn't R.J. want to be my son? Then, with all of your help, I came to realize that this certainly wasn't about *me*. It was about *my child*. And if I didn't get with the program there was a chance that Gloria and I could be planning a funeral. *(He glances at Sally and Ben)* Sorry!

BEN. No worries. We know what you meant.

RICHARD. Anyway, I got with the program, better late than never. Riley is doing better every day. His….sorry, *her* grades are staying up and her friends are unbelievably supportive. I just wanted to say, for both of us, thank you for helping us. The outcome could have been so very different.

(From stage left, **ALLIE** *enters.* **HER** *posture is defeated,* **HER** *hair unkempt and* **SHE** *shuffles with despair. The other* **WOMEN** *rise and rush to* **HER**, *embracing* **HER** *as one.* **SHE** *begins to weep. The* **WOMEN** *guide* **HER** *to a chair.*)

ALLIE. *(Regaining control, wiping her eyes.)* I'm sorry if I'm interrupting the meeting. I know I'm late but I wasn't even certain I would come… *(She trails off.)*

SALLY. Don't even think about it, Allie. You're always welcome here, whenever you can make it.

SUSIE. I know I speak for all of us when I say that we are devastated by your loss. *(Eyes shining with tears.)* Cliché as it might sound, we are truly here for you. And you can call any of us any time, day or night.

(Murmurs of assent from **EVERYONE**.*)*

GLORIA. Do you want to tell us? Talk about it?
ALLIE. Yes, I really need to. Maggie... *(She dabs her eyes once again.)* She began having panic attacks. One day, shortly after I was last here at group, she had a particularly bad one. When I got her calmed down she looked into my eyes with such utter despair...

(Beat.)

She asked me, 'Mom, when I die will I come back as a girl?' I told her yes, absolutely. 'You promise, Mom?' she asked. I said yes, that God would never do that to her. That somehow, this time, he got it wrong. When I look back to that conver-sation I realize that she might have been asking my permission to die. But at the time, since we'd had so many open conversations before, I didn't put any special emphasis on it. I should have realized....

*(***SALLY***, sitting next to ***ALLIE***, takes ***HER*** hand.)*

SALLY. You were doing everything you could, Allie. Sometimes, like Ben and I, it isn't enough and they slip away.
ALLIE. *(Looking around the group in despair.)* I did everything...I really did. We changed her name at school. We had the principal and counselor there on board. She could wear whatever clothing she wanted. Her hair was growing out... *(Tears begin to flow down her cheeks.)* It was so lovely. *(Beat.)* We went to a physiatrist twice a week who specializes in transgender teens. We talked for hours, Maggie and I.

She knew I was saving for any transition surgery that she might want. In six months she was to begin puberty blockers to buy her some time.

*(***SHE*** begins to sob.)*

Then one evening I came home after I'd pulled a double shift. I found her in the bathtub, her wrists.... *(She stops, can't go on.)*

*(***SALLY*** puts ***HER*** arm around ***ALLIE***. ***SUSIE*** rises, crosses, and kneels in front of ***ALLIE***'s chair, holding ***HER*** hands. The ***MEN*** stare at the floor or anywhere except at ***ALLIE***.)*

SALLY. Stop, Allie. You don't have to say it.
SUSIE. She's right, Allie. I am so very sorry, dear, dear girl.

ALLIE. *(Looking up with drenched eyes.)* God couldn't possibly get it wrong a second time, could he? He'll send her back as a girl just like I promised. Won't he?

CURTAIN

THE PERFUME BOTTLE

CAST OF CHARACTERS

Violet - A nine year old. She is the younger
sister of Ivah.

Ivah - An eleven year old, she is the prankster of the family.

Widow Pruitt - A mean old lady who gets the girls into trouble.

Scene One

At Rise: A farm, the backyard.

*(Two sisters, **VIOLET** and **IVAH**, age nine and eleven are cutting branches from a bush.)*

VIOLET. I hate the widow Pruitt!

IVAH. She's a big ole tattle tale!

VIOLET. She's just a big baby! Can't she take a joke?

IVAH. (*Giggles.*) How were we to know that she was in the outhouse when we tipped it over?

VIOLET. Then she had to go and tell Mama.

IVAH. It was an accident. It's not fair. Eddie and Earl didn't get caught. How could they think that we could tip it over by ourselves?

VIOLET. (*Teary.*) And now we're gonna get a switchin'...

IVAH. Oh, now Vi, it's not so bad. You know Mama thinks the biggest part of our punishment is pickin' out the switch she's gonna use on us. She never hits very hard....I hardly feel it.

VIOLET. (*Giggling and sniffling at the same time.*) I know. Mama's such a softy. When she gets upset with me and all kinda' hurt acting; well it's worse than any ole' switching...

IVAH. Well, we're gonna get ole lady Pruitt back....but good!

VIOLET. Oooh. (*Gleefully.*) What're we gonna do, Ivah?

IVAH. You'll see. When's Mama cookin' ham hocks and navy beans next?

VIOLET. Saturday night, why?

IVAH. (*Sagely.*) You'll see. Come on... we gotta get our saved up money and get down to the Five N' Dime before Mr. Golden closes.

VIOLET. Why?

IVAH. You'll see....

*(**THEY** exit and re-enter from across the stage. As they enter VIOLET is saying....)*

VIOLET. Ivy...

IVAH. Don't call me Ivy, I'm not a plant!

VIOLET. Why do we have to use my favorite hair ribbons? I've only worn them once.

IVAH. 'Cause this gift is for the widow Pruitt and it's gotta be perfect...did you bring the bottle?

VIOLET. Yes...and the old cork outta Pa's work bench.

IVAH. And the stationary and envelope?

VIOLET. *(Pulling them out of her pocket.)* Do you think Mama will notice I took these? They're her best.

IVAH. No. *(Taking the cork.)* Good work, little sister.

VIOLET. Don't call me 'little'. I'm almost ten and I'm taller than you.

IVAH. Okay, okay...now give me the bottle and stand back!

> *(IVAH goes behind a bush or tree and there is the sound of farting. VIOLET begins to gasp and giggle and scream.)*

VIOLET. Oh, oh, stop, Ivy! I can smell you clear out here! My eyes are watering.

IVAH. *(Giggling.)* I told you to stand back. It's not my fault, Mama's beans always does this to me.

VIOLET. But Mama says that she cooks them upside down so we'll belch instead of....*(Beat.)*...well, you know...

IVAH. Fart? She just says that so we'll eat 'em.

> *(VIOLET giggles. IVAH comes out from where SHE has hidden, smoothing down her skirt.)*

Now, where's that ribbon?

VIOLET. Right here.

IVAH. Now, we'll tie this beautiful bow around the top, like this....and then write the message on the stationary....let's see, what should it say?

VIOLET. Why do you get to write it? I want to do something.

IVAH. Because I have beautiful handwriting....everyone says so.

VIOLET. *(Whines.)* But, you get to do everything....what do I get to do?

IVAH. Oh, for goodness sakes, Vi, we're using your ribbons, aren't we? *(Beat.)* Oh, all right. You decide what we should say.

VIOLET. Let's see....'a special something for the big, ole, fat, tattletale.'

IVAH. *(Sarcastic.)* Oh that's great.... should we sign it too, 'Love, Ivah and Violet Guyer' while we're at it?

VIOLET. We can't do that, Ivy! Then Mama will find out.... *(Finally gets it.)* Oh...

IVAH. It's gotta be a message....like from a gentleman caller...less 'see...what would Rudolf Valentino say to Claire Bow?

VIOLET. *(laughs.)* 'I love you....I can't live without you....I'll die without you'… *(more giggles.)*

IVAH. I know. 'From a secret admirer...who worships you from afar'.

VIOLET. Oooo....that's good. Write that.

> *(IVAH turns VIOLET around and uses her back to write the message.)*

IVAH. *(Writing.)* 'From a....secret admirer... who....worships you....from afar'... there! Some of my best penmanship, if I do say so.

VIOLET. That's really pretty, Ivy. Now what?

IVAH. The method of delivery. *(Beat.)* Mama would hear us if we snuck out after bedtime so that's no good. I know. Early morning, before anyone is up, I'll have a nature call and pretend to go out to the wash shed. Then I'll run over to the widow Pruitt's and leave it on her porch.

VIOLET. I wanna come.

IVAH. You can't.

VIOLET. But, I want to. *(Whining.)* I never get to do nothin'.

IVAH. 'Anything.' 'Nothin' is bad grammar. We used your hair ribbons, didn't we? Besides, I'm saving the very best for you, Vi.

VIOLET. *(Suspicious.)* What?

IVAH. After we do the breakfast dishes you and I will go over to ole lady Pruitt's and hid in the bushes and watch until she finds the perfume bottle.

VIOLET. We will?

IVAH . Yep. Now, come on....and not a word to Lillas or LaVerne.

VIOLET. Cross my heart *(Doing the motions.)* and hope to die, stick a needle in my eye.

> *(**THEY** exit. Then re-enter. **THEY** are sneaking through the bushes outside the Pruitt home.)*

VIOLET. *(Whispering.)* Where's the perfume bottle? I can't see it. Oh, no, it's gone. She's already found it...

IVAH. *(Whispering.)* Shhh....she'll hear you, dummy. It's there. See? Over by the flower pot?

VIOLET. Oh, yeah.

IVAH. Stay down and be quiet.

VIOLET. I am. *(Beat.)* How long do you think we have to wait?

IVAH. *(Gleefully.)* As long as it takes.

> *(Several beats. The front door opens of **MRS. PRUITT'S** house and a middle aged woman comes out onto the porch. Her hair is up in rollers and she wears an old, torn bathrobe. She has old slippers on.)*

> *(**SHE** takes a deep breath of morning air.)*

WIDOW PRUITT. Ahhh!

> *(Stretching and looking out at the beautiful morning. **SHE** picks up her broom and lazily sweeps the porch. **SHE** sees the pretty perfume bottle.)*

WIDOW PRUITT. Oh my, what do we have here?

WIDOW PRUITT. *(picking the bottle and envelope up.)* Isn't this lovely? Oh, and a note...

> *(**SHE** holds the bottle in her arm as **SHE** tears open the envelope and reads aloud.)*

'From a secret admirer'....Oh my...

>   *(**SHE** fans herself with the envelope and then continues to reads.)*

...who worships you from afar'. Oh my!

>   *(Blushing **SHE** looks around to see if anyone is witness to this declaration of love. **SHE** tucks the love letter and envelope in her robe next to her heart. **SHE** uncorks the bottle and takes a deep inhale of the 'perfume', chokes, gasps and faints from the fumes. **IVAH** and **VIOLET** begin to giggle and then to laugh hysterically.)*

VIOLET. Shhh...shh.   She's....gonna....hear us.

IVAH. *(Laughing hysterically.)*   Ole lady Pruitt can't hear a thing....oh, no, I'm gonna pee my pants....Oh, Oh, that's the funniest thing I ever did see....

VIOLET. *(Sobering, she whispers.)*   You don't think she's dead, do you Ivy? Your farts are really stinky.

IVAH. No, no... just fainted. She's swooned over her secret lover.

VIOLET. She looks dead to me...

IVAH. *(Laughing.)*   You are too serious for nine years old, ya know that, Vi? If you're so worried about her, go poke her to see if she's breathing.

VIOLET. Uh-uh. I'm not going up there.

IVAH. That's what I thought.   Come on, let's get outta here before she wakes up.

IVAH. You know what the worst part is, Vi?

VIOLET. No, what?

IVAH. We can't tell anybody....how are we gonna keep *this* a secret?

>   *(**THEY** exit.)*

CURTAIN

IVAH THE TERRIBLE

CAST OF CHARACTERS

Arthur - He is a successful attorney.

Ivah - Ivah is NOT your typical housewife.

Mr. Hudson - The important client from Chicago.

Jimmy, Paperboy - Young boy.

Scene One

At Rise: The living room of an upscale home.

*(A door leads to the kitchen. It is dinner time at the home of attorney, **ARTHUR GIBBONS** and his wife, Ivah. **ARTHUR** enters the front   door. He wears a suit and carries a briefcase. As he enters, **IVAH** enters from the kitchen. Ivah is in shorts, dirt stains on her legs from working in the garden.)*

ARTHUR. Hi, Doll.   I'm home from the salt mines, finally.
IVAH. Hi honey. *(SHE crosses to him and kisses him.)*   How was court today? Did Judge Ratchet give you the contingency you needed?
ARTHUR. *(Embraces her.)* Yes, thank God. He's a good old bird underneath all that rough talk. Lord, Ivah, what are you wearing? Eu' de' Manure? I love you, but you stink! Digging in the garden today?
IVAH. Yep! *(SHE crosses to a drinks cart. Pours ARTHUR a sherry.)*   And that's where you and I disagree, my love. I adore the smell of freshly turned earth. Then add a little manure for spice....Umm.... *(SHE hands HIM the drink. ARTHUR crosses to HIS chair, pulling off HIS tie, and sits.)*
ARTHUR. You can take the girl out of the country but you can't take the manure off of the girl. *(Beat.)*   And I wouldn't change you for the world.
IVAH. *(Laughing.)*   That's 'backwoods' to you, mister.   I'm no farmer's daughter, even though you like to think so...I'm a woodsmen's daughter through and through and proud of it!
ARTHUR. Oh, please, allow me my dreams. I've always wanted to flirt with a farmer's daughter and right now you smell... *(Laughs.)* exactly how I would imagine she would smell.   Better go get cleaned up. I have an important client dropping in to sign some papers.
IVAH. Oh, Arty. I've got dinner on. Can't he come by the office tomorrow?
ARTHUR. No can do, sweetheart. He's on his way to the airport to catch the red eye back to Chicago. This is our only time to wind this up. Sorry. He won't stay long.
 IVAH. In that case, I'm going to hide in the kitchen until he's gone. I don't have time to clean up before dinner. We'll eat in the kitchen tonight. *(SHE starts to exit, then turns back.)* Chicago? Is this the guy who's so secretive? The one that's loaded with money?
ARTHUR. You have such a turn of phrase.   Yes, he's the one...from Chicago...likes his privacy and if having millions is being 'loaded' then yes, it's the client you're thinking of.

IVAH. Oh, darn...I've always wanted to meet a real live multi-millionaire. Especially this one! He's so mysterious....I'm dying to see him.

ARTHUR. *(Laughs.)* Well, you can't...looking and *smelling* like that.

IVAH. Another time, then.

> *(Crosses to the cart, pours HERSELF a sherry, crosses to the kitchen door.)*

I'll take myself and my sherry out to the kitchen and wait for you there. Hurry it up so dinner isn't ruined.

ARTHUR. He should be here any minute. I have the papers all ready for his signature. Ten minutes tops, love.

IVAH. See you in a bit, darling.

> **(SHE** *exits.* **ARTHUR** *lays the documents on the coffee table, sorting them briefly. The doorbell rings.* **ARTHUR** *rises, crosses to the door and opens it.)*

ARTHUR. Mr. Hudson, sir. Please come in.

> **(MR. HUDSON** *enters, wearing a dark suit and red tie.* **HE** *carries a briefcase.)*

MR. HUDSON. Arthur. Thank you for letting me stop by.

ARTHUR. It's my pleasure, sir. Won't you be seated?

> **(THEY** *cross to the living room.)*

The sofa there is quite comfortable.

MR. HUDSON. Just for a moment. *(Sits. Looking around the room.)* Very nice home you have, Arthur.

ARTHUR. Thank you. May I offer you a drink, sir? Perhaps a sherry?

MR. HUDSON. A small one perhaps.

> **(ARTHUR** *crosses to the drinks tray and pours a glass.* **HE** *crosses back to* **MR. HUDSON.***)*

ARTHUR. This is from Portugal. Quite a decent vintage.

MR. HUDSON. Thank you. I don't have much time. My flight's at eight. I have my driver waiting.

> **(ARTHUR** *sits.)*

ARTHUR. Yes, sir. Here are the papers you asked me to prepare. I believe you will find everything in order.

MR. HUDSON. Excellent. I don't have time to read them in detail. I trust you have followed my instructions to the letter, Arthur?

ARTHUR. Precision Tool and Dye will be acquired on the first of the month, for a purchase price of one point eight million, payable over the next two years. The purchaser's name will be the corporate name and nowhere on the documents does your name appear. Upper management has agreed to stay on for at least the next twelve months. If you will sign here.... *(Turning the pages.)* and here.....and here....

*(As **ARTHUR** is shuffling the papers, there is a soft, tentative knock at   the front door. **ARTHUR** rises.)*

ARTHUR. Excuse me, Sir.

*(**ARTHUR** crosses to the door and opens it.)*

Oh! Hello, there, Jimmy.

*(The paperboy, **JIMMY,** hands **ARTHUR** the evening paper.)*

JIMMY. Hi, Mr. Gibbons.
ARTHUR. Thank you.

*(The **BOY** stands there waiting.)*

What can I do for you?
JIMMY. Collecting for the newspaper delivery, sir.
ARTHUR. Can you come back tomorrow, Jimmy? I'm in the middle of something at the moment.
JIMMY. Gee, Mr. Gibbons I'm late turning in my money. I have to get it all in by tomorrow. If you could....
ARTHUR. Oh, all right. How much is it, son?
JIMMY. Three bucks....er...dollars, Sir.

*(**ARTHUR** takes **HIS** wallet out and gives **JIMMY** a five dollar bill.)*

ARTHUR. Keep the change, Jimmy.
JIMMY. *(Looking at the two dollar tip.)*   Golly, Geez, Mr. Gibbons....

ARTHUR. I appreciate good work, son.
JIMMY. Thanks a lot. Bye...
ARTHUR. You're welcome.

*(**ARTHUR** closes the door with a firm slam and crosses to living   room. **HE** sits.)*

I am so sorry, Mr. Hudson.

MR. HUDSON. I heard. These youngsters today...always leaving everything to the last minute. Reminds me of my grandson. I believe I've signed everything. Best if you go through and double check....make certain you have what you need. I am most eager to complete this purchase.
ARTHUR. Yes, sir, of course.

> *(***ARTHUR*** *takes the documents and begins to go through them.* **HIS** *head is down.* **MR.
> HUDSON** *sits back, and glances around. The kitchen door silently swings open to reveal*
> **IVAH** *on her hands and knees, crawling through the doorway.* **SHE** *is still in her
> gardening shorts, her hair is askew and there are smudges of dirt on her legs and arms. As*
> **MR. HUDSON** *watches,* **IVAH** *crawls across the dining room floor, with great stealth.*
> **SHE** *crawls to the large bay window and, still on her knees,* **SHE** *cautiously parts the
> sheers and peeps out to get a look at the mysterious client who* **SHE** *thinks has just left.*
> **ARTHUR** *looks up,* **HIS** *attention focused on HIS client and the papers.* **HE** *has not
> seen* **IVAH**.*)*

ARTHUR. These look fine, Mr. Hudson. I will record them tomorrow and wire the first installment....

> *(***MR. HUDSON*** *bursts out laughing.* **ARTHUR** *looks stunned. At* **ARTHUR***'s voice and
> the sound of laughter,* **IVAH** *whirls around, aghast when* **SHE** *sees Mr. Hudson still
> seated in the living room.* **MR. HUDSON** *laughs harder.* **IVAH** *starts to grin.* **ARTHUR**
> *turns and sees* **IVAH,** *for the first time, kneeling by the window.)*

ARTHUR. Ivah! My God, what are you doing?

> *(***MR. HUDSON*** *continues to chuckle.* **IVAH** *brazenly grins at Mr. Hudson.)*

IVAH. Trying to get a good look at....well...at you! Would you like to stay for dinner?

CURTAIN

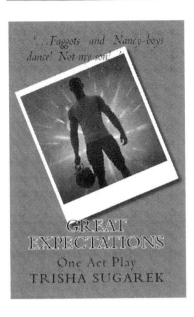

More of the 10 minute plays ideal for the classroom. Visit www.writeratplay.com, www.Amazon.com or other fine book stores.

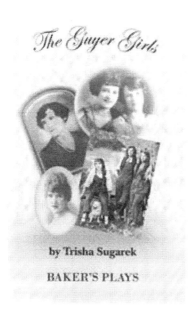

Available at www.amazon.com and your favorite book stores.

31984044R00094

Printed in Great Britain
by Amazon